CHRISTMAS *with* Victoria

VOLUME V

Text by Terry Trucco

Oxmoor
HOUSE®

HEARST COMMUNICATIONS, INC.

Christmas with Victoria, *Volume V*

Oxmoor House, Inc.
Book Division of Southern Progress Corporation
P.O. Box 2463, Birmingham, AL 35201

ISBN: 0-8487-2439-9
ISSN: 1093-7633

Printed in Singapore
First printing 2001

We're here for you!
We at Oxmoor House are dedicated to serving you with reliable information that expands your imagination and enriches your life. We welcome your comments and suggestions. Please write us at:
Oxmoor House, Inc.
Christmas with Victoria
2100 Lakeshore Drive
Birmingham, AL 35209
To order additional publications, call (205) 877-6560 or visit us at www.oxmoorhouse.com

For *Victoria* Magazine
Editor in Chief: Margaret Kennedy
Creative Director: Cynthia Hall Searight
www.victoriamag.com

Editor: Bruce Shostak
Designer: Lynne Yeamans

Produced by Smallwood & Stewart, Inc., New York

Contents

Foreword

If you're like me, you look for holiday inspiration everywhere, all year long. However, as Christmas approaches, I find that my main list keeps sprouting more lists! Always, there are new recipes I've

tucked away to try, especially for the cookie presents I bake every year for family and friends. And the gift list—it isn't just a matter of rushing around at the last minute and checking off names. Thinking ahead, I tend to stock up on unusual presents I discover on my travels. But I also delight in finding a clever trick for charming wrappings, unearthing just the right favor for every guest at a small party, and setting aside the time to make that one personalized creation for someone special. And don't you think that decking the halls always seems more fun when you experiment with fresh ideas?

Our wish is that every moment of anticipating and celebrating the holidays holds joy for you, as it does for all of us at *Victoria.* To spur your own creativity, we've gathered together our most celebratory ideas in this book. Yes, you'll find handmade ornaments, such as the ribbon balls that may inspire you to spend a giddy afternoon in the ribbon shop. Yes, every year we collect more recipes, decorating touches, and ideas for comfortable but festive entertaining. But we also collect the many moods of Christmas: nostalgic, pastoral, elegant, or, my favorite this year, pretty.

Of course, the best mood of all is happy and grateful. I hope you'll be as thrilled with all you can take away from these pages as we are to share our holiday spirit with you.

Wishing you peace,

Peggy Kennedy

Editor in Chief, *Victoria*

All the Trimmings

❖ dressy ribbon ornaments

❖ handmade favor cartons

❖ fancy-cuff stockings

❖ mother-of-pearl button gifts

❖ presents in special frames

❖ greenery and ribbon bow

❖ dessert-table magic

TRIMMINGS ARE RARELY CALLED PRACTICAL, BUT dressmakers and milliners know better: They understand that a slip of ribbon, crochet, or ruffle is as potent as an exotic spice. At Christmas, especially, trimmings can elevate even the humblest object, for they have a joyful spirit that makes us smile. Who hasn't saved a beaded leaf or a silk flower bud from an old hat just because it's so pretty?

Milliners' and dressmakers' trimmings are wonderfully surprising treats for the eye, perhaps because not many of us expect them to adorn the presents or the tree. But dressed with a few flirtatious snippets, your gifts and decorations will be as stunning as a hat by Lilly Daché.

Our frosty pastel decorations and wrappings inspired by the millinery world are a refreshing, yet still wintry, twist on the traditional green and red.

New trimmings are fairly easy to find. Sewing shops and millinery supply stores are treasure houses, piled high with all you need to add charming touches to your entire house for the holidays—inexpensive cords, tiny nosegays, decorative buttons, beaded flowers, floral fabrics of cotton and silk. If you enjoy a good hunt, head for flea markets and secondhand stores; keep your eyes open all throughout the year, and your basket of supplies will be full before Thanksgiving.

Now, begin. Pin a Styrofoam ball with ribbons, and it turns into an alluring heirloom ornament. Let tiny milliner's bouquets bring the kiss of spring to a wrapped gift, a garland, or a shade pull. We were so taken with milliner's ephemera that we adorned a tree with miniature hatboxes, each tied with a narrow ribbon. Soft, delightfully feminine, and utterly romantic, a milliner's Christmas can be uniquely your own, a signature statement at once timeless and chic.

RIBBON ROSETTES AND FLORAL BUNDLES *Flowers that bloom in winter are like tiny miracles, even when they're fashioned from ribbon or silk. To create presents that evoke a fragrant bouquet, packages are wrapped in vintage floral fabric and tied with milliner's flowers in lieu of bows (opposite). Rosettes, made from fabric gathered to resemble roses, first appeared in the eighteenth century as badges of honor. Ours, stitched from ribbon and ribbon rosettes, are so versatile and pretty they can trim a tree (above), dress up a package (left), or even adorn a little girl's hat during the holidays. To learn how to make them, turn to page 131.*

DRESSY RIBBON
ORNAMENTS
*Orbs of shimmering
ribbons (this page and
opposite) are the only
lights needed on a
blue spruce anchored
in an antique urn.
The ornaments are
made using Styrofoam
balls, ribbon, and
sequin pins. Choose a
color scheme, then
combine ribbons and
trims differently on
each ball. Give your
presents that same
sense of variety by
not wrapping any two
alike. Instructions
for the ornaments are
on page 130.*

FANCY-PAPER FAVOR CARTONS
Created in the shape of vintage candy boxes found at a Paris market, our paper-trimmed cartons (this page) are cut from poster board and can be covered with wrapping paper, wallpaper, or color photocopies of old journals or fashion illustrations. Use them as you would a stocking or a little felt gift sack; fancifully wrapped favors and old-fashioned chocolate coins (opposite, top) fulfill the promise tied in the pink grosgrain bow. Turn to pages 132 and 136 for the instructions and templates.

Crafting heavenly presents
and ornaments, we recall all
the dreamy qualities of
the season. Fill a stocking or
a little sack with candies
and gifts, and you'll
fill it with memories that
will last all year.

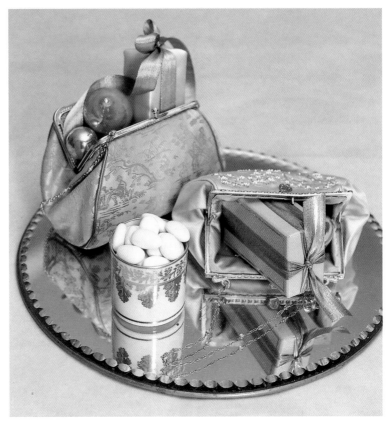

EVENING-BAG "STOCKINGS"

Tuck small gifts and ornaments into elegant little purses (right), and the wrapping becomes part of the present. Evening bags brimming with treats make glamorous favors for a very special Christmas luncheon or tea. Place a purse on each guest's plate or hang one from every chair back. The handbags can be vintage or new; these were created with old purse frames and several new fabrics.

SIMPLE STOCKINGS, FANCY CUFFS

If fashioned from a lovely fabric, a stocking may need no further embellishment than an unexpected profile or a whimsical trimming. The graceful fan-shaped cuff of a stocking in palest icy teal (opposite) is emphasized by an edging of narrow velvet ribbon. A slender stocking (this page) looked almost prim until we added a flounce made from a gathered silk sash salvaged from a turn-of-the-century dress. Both stockings are silk charmeuse, a supple fabric known for its undulant drape. See pages 133–137 for templates and instructions.

BUTTON-TOPPED BOX

Decorate a gift with pearly buttons, and everything shimmers. Arranged with holes facing every which way, cream-colored buttons of different sizes and designs sparkle like a dusting of snowflakes on the lid of a handmade gift box (left), ideal for jewelry, stamps, and—especially—buttons. The box and its lid are lined in ecru silk, then wrapped on the outside with a page photocopied from an antique book. The buttons are attached with glue. To keep every inch on view, we tied it all up in a sheer organdy ribbon.

BUTTONED-UP BOOKMARK

It doesn't take very many buttons to craft a keepsake. Adorned with seven broad buttons, each carved in a different pattern, a satin ribbon (right) is transformed into a bookmark fit for a first edition. Allow extra ribbon for the fringe: To create it, unravel and knot the ribbon's threads at both ends.

BUTTON-TRIMMED TOWEL *A linen fingertip towel (below) gets an opalescent stripe from a tight procession of buttons. The buttons are stitched to a border with silk thread, doubled for extra strength. Mother-of-pearl buttons are so pretty, they deserve to be kept in plain sight— in storage jars, trumpet vases, or shallow bowls.*

FABRIC FRAME

The gift of a treasured old photograph is more special if presented in a frame inspired by the picture itself. Ours (left) is made by gluing fabric and trim reminiscent of the summer dresses worn by the girls in the picture to a piece of framing mat cut with an oval opening.

SHELL PICTURE

A heart created from souvenirs of summer at the beach (opposite) will elicit a smile in the cold of winter. Place the shells in a heart shape, with smaller shells at the edges, and cut a piece of heavy cardboard to fit the shape. Using a glue gun, affix the shells to the board, working from the outside in and layering shells to hide the cardboard. Our shell heart is attached to a ground of natural linen, then matted and framed to finish the gift.

As trees stand bare and the air turns frosty, bring Christmas indoors. Tie a ribbon to a wreath, drape a garland over a window. Then light the candles, and embrace family and friends.

GREENERY AND RIBBON BOW

Mix tones and textures of greenery as you deck the halls. Two bundles of blue spruce and seeded eucalyptus (above), secured to each other with floral wire and finished in the center with satin ribbon tails, make an elegant but spirited topknot for an antique oval looking glass.

RIBBON TABLE RUNNERS

Ribbons infuse everything with a festive glow during the holidays. Instead of using traditional tablecloths or runners, you can transform ultrawide ribbon for your needs with just a few snips. A lustrous pair of runners (right) is created by draping two strands of satin ribbon over a small table. Using pinking shears—to provide a petticoat flourish and keep the ends from unraveling—cut the ribbon into lengths that float just an inch or two above the floor.

SHIMMERING DESSERT TABLE

A table set for a little dessert and Champagne can have all the glamour and magic of a dining room set to the nines. Here, vintage pink ornaments, piled high in a Paris porcelain fruit basket, provide a gaily twinkling centerpiece. Early-nineteenth-century French candelabra, pushed shoulder to shoulder, look grander here than on a long dinner table. The setting, though small, is certainly fit for a celebration.

Nature's Ornaments

- ❖ winter branch arrangements
- ❖ dried lavender wreath
- ❖ giant bay leaf wreath
- ❖ sweetly scented sachets
- ❖ pinecone luminarias
- ❖ star anise and clove balls

OST OF US BRING ARMLOADS OF GREENERY into the house at Christmas, but the holiday spirit blooms just as vibrantly in some of winter's seemingly sparse offerings. In a snowy field, graceful bare branches stretch to embrace the sky. Small dots of color cheer us—red barberries, crimson rose hips, purple privet berries, and yellow bittersweet pods. Even in winter, when the flower garden slumbers, no one knows how to decorate quite like Mother Nature.

And how very wise she is. Decorating with branches, pods, and berries brings a welcome serenity and dignity to a house during this season of razzle-dazzle. Half the fun is in the gathering, whether out in

Fill your basket with everything you fancy, from boxwood sprigs to tiny hemlock pinecones. No gift from nature is too small to bring good cheer.

the woods or right in the backyard, for you never know exactly what might turn up. Perhaps you'll find an abandoned bird's nest, waiting to be filled with a fancifully wrapped gift or tiny glass balls. Or a shapely bough with leaves and nuts clinging to it like ornaments will be the unexpected adornment for a sideboard. Maybe you'll come away with only a handful of boxwood and stand a pert sprig in each pane of a window, so that your good wishes extend to all who look in.

Working with fragrant plant materials is a wonderful way to spend a chilly day. Bundle fresh bay leaves into a wreath (it will last until Easter). Or brew a potpourri from a sixteenth-century recipe of oils and dried flowers. After all, who needs to venture outside when you've already carried the best of everything indoors?

BRANCHING OUT *Once the silkiest leaves and flowers disappear, nature's prowess as a sculptor goes on display. Even in a vase, long crab apple branches laden with small fruits (opposite) maintain the joyous arc of a tree. Sleek branches give height and airiness to a bounteous bouquet (above) of lady apples, green figs still on their twigs, a pomegranate, and the red berry clusters of Sargent's rowan. Reclining along a rustic mantel (right), a single branch pruned from an oak tree, numerous acorns still attached, is a stunning, impromptu work of art.*

PARADING PEARS

A free-form tabletop arrangement (right) pays homage to the pear—real, faux, and framed—with compliments to the partridge in a pear tree. Dressing the scene for the holidays, eucalyptus sprigs flutter here and there.

BLOOMS AND GREENERY

Sometimes Christmas greens need a lift. Snowy white tulips (opposite) bring spring's unexpected caress to a profuse bunch of seeded eucalyptus in a 1930s Italian painted vase.

LAVENDER AND RIBBON WREATH

*One wreath (above) is made by attaching small
bunches of dried lavender stems, each one
bundled with upholstery thread or transparent
nylon thread, to a wire wreath form. A spiral
of ribbon is the final touch. Since lavender
crumbles when excessively dry, wreaths should
hang where there is humidity or move from
time to time to a steamy bathroom. A few drops
of lavender oil, applied carefully, will renew
the blooms' sweet floral fragrance.*

BAY LEAF WREATH
*As if being luscious
to look at weren't enough, an enormous wreath
of fresh bay leaves (right) gives off a clean, spicy
scent that grows more vibrant as the leaves dry.
Hundreds of leaves are gathered into little
bunches tied with light wire or waxed florist
twine, then attached to a sturdy wire wreath
form. For a sumptuous variation, blend bay
with boxwood, holly, ivy, and rosemary.*

CHOOSING HERBAL POTPOURRIS

*In Elizabethan times, a mix of dried bay leaves,
marigold, mint, lavender, and herbs (opposite)
was scattered on the floor to release a heavenly
scent when crushed underfoot. A potpourri
for a kitchen or a dining room should have a
fruity or spicy scent rather than a floral one,
to complement the aromas of food.*

mixing elizabethan sachets

The English ruled by Good Queen Bess understood the value and versatility of fragrant herbs and spices. Barks, greens, leaves, flowers, and oils were strewn over floors, hung from the rafters, and mixed into potpourris to keep the house smelling sweet. Following a recipe borrowed from a tiny shop in London's East End, where such sixteenth-century herbal favorites as nutmeg, cloves, dried lavender, and marigold (opposite) are used, you can mix a modern-day variation of sweet bags (below). Visit a botanicals shop for the ingredients.

OILS

120 drops (6 milliliters) rose scent
   (or rose-scented oil)

80 drops (4 milliliters) sandalwood oil

40 drops (2 milliliters) frankincense oil

20 drops (1 milliliter) myrrh

10 drops (½ milliliter) black pepper oil

BOTANICALS

¼ ounce powdered orrisroot

¼ ounce powdered gum benzoin

10 ounces dried rose petals
   (highly scented ones are best)

1 ounce whole cloves

2 ounces allspice berries, crushed

1 cinnamon stick, broken into
   small pieces

Blend the oils together in a bowl. In another bowl, mix together the orrisroot and the gum benzoin. Stir in the oils a bit at a time. The mixture will be pastelike. Add the remaining botanicals, stirring well until everything is coated. Cover the bowl and store it in a dark place for a few days to mature. Fill small cloth pouches with the mixture, tie them closed with ribbon, and give them as gifts or use them in your own home.

NOTE: It's not necessary to add all the oil, which is very pungent. Stored in a dark bottle, leftover oil can refresh the bags as the fragrance fades.

A textured and aromatic display (opposite) extends a candlelit welcome. Arranged in a transferware platter, pinecones, pomanders, and a feather are a wintry alternative to flowers. Topping the footed bowl is a fragrant star anise ball. To make it, hot-glue pods of star anise all over a six-inch Styrofoam ball. Poke whole cloves into the empty spaces until the Styrofoam is as obscured as possible. The pods, available at Asian markets, sometimes break, so buy them in bulk. Place extras in a bag with cinnamon sticks, and you'll have a large sachet to keep wherever you'd like to fill the air with spices.

PINECONE LUMINARIAS *When guests are expected, pillar candles framed by alternating boxwood and grapevine wreaths (right) can light the way to the door. As if they had just fallen from a tree, pinecones are generously sprinkled around the wreaths. If the night is windy, place the candles in hurricanes or large glass canning jars to keep the flames from blowing out. A Christmas tree (above) stands unadorned in a concrete planter, enhancing the woodland-inspired fantasy.*

Childhood Memories

- ❖ mitten garland
- ❖ holiday photo displays
- ❖ sewn paper stockings
- ❖ vintage newsprint gift cones
- ❖ secret songs and messages
- ❖ big tree, little tree

THOUGH GROWN-UPS SOMETIMES FORGET, children sense the magic in every moment of Christmas. Spending time with a young child is one way to revisit that fanciful realm of flying reindeer and gifts handpicked by Santa. But so, too, is surrounding yourself with the ephemera of childhood—the toys, tiny garments, snapshots, and curios that are not mere objects but memories.

Little ones will no doubt love everything they see in a house adorned with childhood souvenirs. For adults, it's a holiday fantasy that's as much fun to put together as it is to see. Conjure your happiest memories, then visit the attic, pore over photo albums, and sift through well-stuffed

Decorate with mementos of childhood—woolen mittens, a pair of skates, a rosy button—and you'll reawaken sweet memories while making new ones.

An ornament, a bird's nest,
a baby shoe—which whispers
of Christmas Past to you?

boxes for treasures. The angel that crowned Grandmother's tree, the stocking with your name—yes, they're worthy of display. But mementos don't need a holiday theme to stir recollections at Christmas. Transport yourself back to that ice pageant with a garland strung with mittens. Or dress the mantel with a tiny pair of Mary Janes, tied with jingle bells, in honor of your first chat with Santa.

Use groupings to make an impact. Filled with dollhouse furnishings, baby booties, or marbles and jacks, a dignified silver compote becomes as playful as a five-year-old. Your landscape is of the past, so choose objects that have left behind some of their youthful brashness. The many objects on these pages wear gentle colors and invite all who see them to join in the journey back to Christmas Whenever. It's a pleasing trip, and one that will no doubt provide plenty of warm memories to be savored some Christmas Future.

LOOKING BACK *Happy memories may be our finest heirlooms. Present meets past in a silvery still life (opposite): Compotes hold mittens and tinsel, and a little tree is trimmed with baby shoes. A clothespin (above left) can clip a few mementos almost anywhere. A beribboned vintage lunch box (left) delivers holiday cookies.*

A CLOTHESPIN FOR YOUR THOUGHTS *How sweet to gaze upon fond memories! A gift swathed in 1930s newspaper (opposite) is wrapped, literally, in the past; a snapshot, clipped on with a clothespin, is the bow. In the spirit of stockings, mittens (this page) are hung with clothespins. A bowl overflows with a nostalgic potpourri of cards and notions.*

STITCHED
PAPER
STOCKINGS

Though Christmas stockings always convey tidings of good cheer, our sewn paper versions, clothespinned to a garland of rick-rack and twine (this page), are ideal for easily customized greetings. Use a color photocopier to create a collage of images you like, such as a child's wish list for Santa, a page from a children's Christmas book, family photos, or a snappy print, like the tartan shelf paper from the 1940s (opposite, left) that we used. Hang the stockings from every window or tie them on the tree. They make ideal wrappings for gift certificates or theater tickets. Or use them as place cards, with a poem or a favor tucked inside. See pages 135 and 137 for instructions and a template.

At Christmas, even presents can be black, white, and read all over. Rolled into a cone that's secured with tape in the back, yesterday's news makes a handsome, and literate, gift container (below) to hang from a doorknob or a mantel, particularly if the headlines date from a Christmas past. For a cone sturdy enough to hold a supply of small gifts, use several sheets of folded paper. Wire a jingle bell to the tip and hang with a length of ribbon or tinsel garland.

Paper can be transformed into anything, from cards to wrappings

to ornaments. What a fitting symbol of the season's ephemeral beauty.

CHRISTMAS SEALS *Memorable gift tags (left) are easy to make with a rubber stamp that reproduces an image from an old book or from a child's drawing. You can also use the stamp to seal the flaps of envelopes or to adorn paper ornaments. Or give a custom stamp, with an ink pad, as a gift. Choose your image, then visit a stationer to order a custom rubber stamp.*

TABLETOP NOEL *Write a merry message with colorful cord (opposite) atop any table. The nubby surface of an old linen dish towel, draped as a runner, holds the sentiment in place; if you want permanence, stitch the writing to the cloth by hand. Stoneware bottles, a jar ruffed with rickrack, and a flea-market tumbler are vases for candy canes and twigs tied with tiny pinecones.*

SECRET SONG WRAPPINGS
Just twelve inches wide and often available at flea markets, obsolete rolls of paper player-piano music are fun for wrapping small gifts. The perforations that once activated piano keys still sing out if the present is wrapped first in colored paper. If you can't keep a secret, add a card naming the tune; our packages (right) wear "L'amour, Toujours L'amour."

A Theme for Two Trees

What child, young or old, hasn't dreamed of having a Christmas tree, or two, or three, in every room? Instead of a giant showstopper, one homeowner fills her house with a series of tabletop trees, from a live blue spruce (left) to a diminutive bottle-brush example from the 1930s (opposite). To complement each other across the room, the two trees share a palette of reds, faded pinks, and creamy whites. The artificial snow sprinkled over the tiny tree is echoed in the homemade snowflakes, chandelier crystals, and looped pipe-cleaner garland embellishing the spruce; the transfer-ware cup holding the miniature tree is a lustreware echo of the printed toile fabric wrapped around the root ball of the spruce.

CHAPTER FOUR

Handcrafted Harvest

❖ snow-frosted votives

❖ burlap gift bundles

❖ clothespin constellations

❖ folk-art ornament collections

❖ paper-cone wall pockets

ERHAPS BECAUSE CHRISTMAS BEGAN, IN ONE sense, in a barn, many of us as the holidays approach long to surround ourselves with the natural materials and homespun goods that we associate with a rustic environment. Few of us may actually spend the holidays in a snowy world, with an old barn to decorate. But as we hang a glistening tin snowflake on the tree or tie a plaid ribbon to the mailbox, our imaginations wander to a rural landscape—one that may or may not still exist—of sleighbells, firelight, and silent nights.

For bringing that gentle, pastoral mood to your home, nothing is more effective than decorations made by hand, whether by you, a child,

Stars of wonder, stars of light: Beautiful sparklers, made of wooden elements or colorful punched tin, can be collected and cherished for seasons to come.

or an artisan. What matters is the human touch that makes each object unlike any other in the world and instills in it a trace of its creator.

Before the advent of manufactured ornaments, artisans crafted holiday decorations from whatever was at hand. Humble materials, such as straw, paper, beeswax, and tin, were rendered into enchanting shapes—and works of folk art. Natural materials, particularly those with rich textures, still make eloquent decorations that can grace any part of an apartment or a house. Adorned with ribbons or braid, rugged burlap looks as luxuriant as velvet and can serve as a witty, and reusable, gift wrap or tree skirt.

Creating the spirit of a rustic holiday, however, can be a simple matter of rearranging the furniture. Tie a big bow to a child's painted rocking chair and place it by the tree. Or hang jingle bells from a much-loved old sled and set it beside the front door. And as you tie a sprig of greenery above the elevator or the garage door, you may, for just a moment, inhale a breath of crisp, clear country air.

RURAL HOLIDAY *Barns seem naturally festive at Christmas, perhaps because they so often wear red. To elevate the holiday mood, an old sled and a bushy fir, adorned with a carved angel (opposite), stand watch at the door. Big plaid gift sacks beneath the tree may be evidence of a thoughtful Santa. More presents arrive by the basketful (right), each package bundled in burlap, tied with twine, and garnished with snips of greenery and cinnamon sticks. A lacy wreath on the door (above) gets its homespun twinkle from a star handwoven of wheat.*

SNOW-FROSTED VOTIVES AND HURRICANES *A single candle beckons through a frosted window. Re-create this holiday icon in miniature by faux-frosting clear-glass hurricanes and votives. We placed ours (this page and opposite) to light unused stairs, but they would be just as cheerful along a mantel. To make them, cut out paper trees and stars, then tape the shapes to the hurricanes. Spray the glass with glue and roll it in artificial snow. Don't strive for perfection; an uneven effect will look more natural. Remove the paper to reveal the silhouettes. Votives are usually too small for silhouettes; just spray and roll. Come January, a hot, soapy bath will remove the frost.*

CLOTHESPIN
STARS *A star
needn't be shiny to
twinkle. Ours, made
from clothespins, light
up a wreath (right)
and assemble as a
constellation in an
arching spray of pine
boughs (below right).
Unadorned, these easy
ornaments have a
Shaker-like simplicity,
though they can be
dressed up with paint
or glitter. All the
supplies are available
at crafts stores. To
make a star, attach
the heads of four
clothespins with wood
glue to a 1½-inch
wooden disk, turning
the pins so the openings
don't show. Glue a
fifth clothespin on its
side with the opening
facing up, then glue
a ½-inch wooden ball
to the center. To hang
a star from a tree, you
can slip the outward-
facing opening over
a branch of greenery.
If you prefer, hot-glue
the midpoint of a
length of plaid ribbon
to the wooden disk,
then tie the star
wherever you wish.*

CLOTHESLINE
GARLAND
*A twine garland
of ornaments hung
with clothespins
(opposite) has a plain
charm befitting a
handcrafted country-
style celebration. These
cinnamon-scented
beeswax ornaments
were molded by
craftswomen; the
antique springerle
molds hung from
colorful ribbon
are just some of the
ones that are used
to make ornaments.*

Whether it's a tin snowflake or a star woven of North Dakota wheat, a handmade ornament has a grace and humanity that no amount of mass-produced sparkle can touch. Fortunately for collectors, the custom of creating ornaments by hand is vibrantly alive. Like the miniature artworks they are, handmade decorations are occasionally signed by an artisan. Often, you can buy ornaments directly from their creators at holiday fairs, such as the annual Chriskindlmarkt in Bethlehem, Pennsylvania, and perhaps pick up a tip or two if you're planning to make a painted wooden Santa or a beeswax maple leaf of your own.

A postcard ornament (opposite, top left) is easy to make. Punch a hole in each of the two top corners, thread cord or narrow ribbon through to form a loop, and knot the ends to keep them secure.

Natural materials blossom when turned into ornaments, like a Moravian star coaxed from straw (opposite, top right).

An antique springerle mold meant for making cookies yielded this beeswax ornament with a painted pinecone design (opposite, bottom left).

Uexpected shapes enliven familiar forms. A slender terra-cotta heart (opposite, bottom right) seems almost to be wearing a smile.

A classic Father Christmas (right) was made by pouring melted beeswax into an antique cookie mold. Beeswax is excellent for making decorations: It lasts for years, and it won't melt unless it's heated to 148 degrees Fahrenheit.

On Christmas Eve,
an imaginative eye sees
stars in the straw and
wreaths in coils of twine.

HAYLOFT INSPIRATIONS *Whether in a barn or a penthouse, an old-fashioned Christmas comes to mind when the tree's branches are laden with handcrafted ornaments (opposite), particularly those made from humble materials, such as straw, paper, and tin. As befits its rustic setting, the tree is skirted with layers of hay. A sled with sleigh bells stands as a work of folk art; a wooden bin keeps all the presents corralled.*

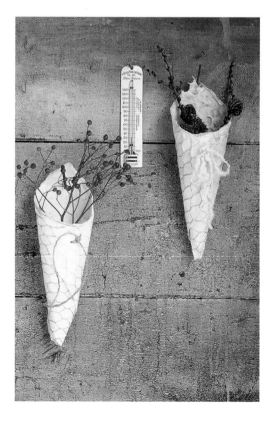

CHRISTMAS COLLAGE *An arrangement of keepsakes (above) can tell a story. Create something similar by pinning cards and ribbons to a bulletin board or setting out treasured toys and homemade ornaments on an entry-hall table.*

PAPER WALL VASES *Inspired by vintage ceramic wall vases, these cones (right) are charming whether they hold arrangements or tiny gifts. We chose handmade paper embossed with chicken wire, but any sturdy paper will do. Roll a ten-inch square into a cone; glue it closed where the edges overlap. Add two holes in front for bows; make one hole in the back for hanging.*

CHAPTER FIVE

Afternoon Open House

* holiday favor boxes
* easy hors d'oeuvres
* spinach and fontina tart
* herb-roasted fillet of beef
* wild-rice salad
* flaky cream biscuits
* old-fashioned lemon bars
* apricot nut cake

W E'LL NEVER KNOW THE NAME OF THE hospitable soul who first invited folks to drop by the house, anytime between two and four, to eat, drink, and mingle. But if we were to guess the season in which such gatherings became customary, it would be Christmas. The decorations are in place. The tree twinkles. And friends and families come together, eager to embrace the new fiancé, play with the little ones, and renew old ties. Is there a better time to have a party?

There certainly are less hectic months of the year to entertain. But whether it's a dessert party with tea and Champagne on a December afternoon or a luxurious lunch buffet on New Year's Day, with good

A party is the best time to play the role of Santa. Send your guests home with soaps or sachets or a wrapped slice of dense apricot nut cake nestled in woven boxes.

planning an open house can accommodate guests of all ages, and will relax and refresh everyone who attends, including you.

Given the hustle-bustle of the holidays, you have every excuse to orchestrate a party that's both elegant and easy. Choose flavorful foods that can be prepared in advance and are no trouble for guests to manage as they balance plates and glasses. Bite-size appetizers from the gourmet store or catalog are the perfect complement to a buffet of assorted salads, sliced meats, and perhaps a casserole or a cheese tart. Set up a sweets table with cookies and cakes and let everyone nibble. And since we all deserve one more present, why not prepare a small gift for each guest? Wrapped in an attractive box, playing cards, pistachio nuts, or candies make agreeable favors for young and old alike. Or you might choose fragrant gifts, such as scented soaps and herbal sachets.

Set everything out before your guests arrive, then let the pleasures of the afternoon begin. This may well become a yearly event.

HOUSE PARTY *Encourage guests to move about and mingle by placing baskets and trays of finger food (opposite and right) throughout the rooms you are using for the gathering. Cheeses, fresh and dried fruits, and bite-size savories such as Japanese rice crackers, sweet-potato chips, and herbed olives are all eye-catching and require no preparation other than a trip to the gourmet market. Better yet, all are most delicious at room temperature. Instead of stacking napkins on the table, tuck them into a glass vase (above) and let them do double duty as a centerpiece.*

Food that's elegant and
easy to manage is ideal
for the casual atmosphere
of an open house.

ARRANGING A WINTER BUFFET
*A gracefully uncrowded buffet (opposite)
contributes to a serene mood. Dress the table
simply with a diaphanous cloth—you could
use yards of inexpensive muslin from the fabric
store and leave the ends unhemmed—and a
generous bouquet of silvery winter greenery.
Set out everything, from napkins to goblets to
salad, so that it's within manageable reach.*

CHOOSING THE MENU *When planning
a buffet meal, choose foods that guests can
transfer from platter to plate without a struggle,
and offer plenty to please everyone, including
vegetarians. An elegant spinach and fontina tart
(above) is a wonderful companion to our wild-
rice salad (opposite). Medaillons of herb-roasted
fillet of beef (right) are easy to serve and elevate
simple fare into a celebration; the accompanying
horseradish sauce can be made ahead of time.
Our flaky biscuits are the epitome of a kitchen
basic that's great for a crowd. Every guest will
be delighted with them, for these days biscuits
are baked at home all too infrequently. To find
the recipes, turn to pages 100–103.*

Every party, grand or small, deserves eye-catching touches meant for every guest, so outfit the table in its holiday best. For a daytime event, we like a winter palette of white, silver, gold, and silvery greens. Since the table shouldn't feel crowded, choose a simple centerpiece: a single bouquet of flowers or a pair of fruit bowls filled with ornaments. To everything you present, add a flourish. Start with the napkins—here are a few ideas:

Standing ready in Champagne flutes, folded napkins and dessert forks (opposite) dress up a sweets table. With a plate of cake in hand, each guest need only pluck a glass off the sideboard.

Handwritten napkin rings (above left) were inspired by fortune cookie messages. First, make a color photocopy of an appropriate passage from an old, beautifully written letter or a book that touches your heart. Using wavy-edged scissors, cut the text in a long rectangle; wrap it around a rolled napkin and tie it with a metallic cord or ribbon.

A bundle of flatware tied with a ruffle of sheer rippled ribbon and centered on a dinner plate (left) is a gift for guests to untie when all have taken their seats. Add a sprig of greenery or a flower, and this elegant package becomes a bouquet.

Napkin rings can be favors in themselves. Attach a ribbon to a small gift, such as a gauzy pouch filled with miniature jelly beans or Jordan almonds, a gingerbread boy or girl in a cellophane bag, or a trio of ball ornaments tied together with a bow, and tie the ribbon around a rolled napkin.

APRICOT NUT CAKE *To orchestrate a preview of the flavors within our moist dessert (this page), we surrounded it with a collar of hazelnuts and dried apricots. Each slice can be served with a drizzle of eggnog sauce. The recipes are on pages 105–106.*

OLD-FASHIONED LEMON BARS *Cut into diamonds, these tangy lemon bars (opposite) are a tempting addition to the familiar parade of holiday cookies. The recipe is on page 104.*

CHAPTER SIX

Winter Feasts

- ❖ traditional turkey dinner
- ❖ warm and hearty soups
- ❖ savory pies
- ❖ iced chocolate mousse
- ❖ chocolate-banana-ginger cake
- ❖ refreshing poached pears

A MEAL IS AN EVERYDAY OCCURRENCE. BUT A feast is an event, particularly in winter, when the tradition of grand-scale dining began. For the early Europeans, December was the season—the only season—for fresh meat, new wine, and a brief respite from agricultural chores. Who wouldn't want to revel? Winter foods are still a satisfying marriage of sustenance and celebration; their robust flavors and familiar aromas remind us that it's time to sit down once again to a beautiful, laden table and feast.

For many of us, a sumptuous Christmas Day repast with a golden turkey, ruby cranberries, and potatoes whipped into creamy peaks defines

Share the season's bounty with friends: Nothing brightens a winter night quite like warm, flavorful comfort foods and morsels of delectable desserts.

"feast" to perfection. But a feast is really anything we want it to be. This season of fancy eating is a perfect time to return to homey foods that warm you on a frosty night. A pre-Christmas Sunday night supper requires nothing more than a delicious soup, ready at the table in a generous tureen. Or why not invite your closest friends over for a casual dinner of shepherd's pie? The holiday season is all about luxurious dining, so our version, made with tender chunks of sirloin or filet mignon, delivers luxury in its unassuming wrapping.

Feasts deserve impressive finales, so serve something grand. An iced chocolate mousse or glazed pears in port wine will delight even well-sated guests. And as they wend their way home, they'll find themselves mulling over an intriguing question: Were the original comfort foods savories or sweets?

KEEPING WITH TRADITION *Turkey is available year-round but always tastes best during the holidays, perhaps because the foods that accompany it most agreeably are in season. Served with roasted chestnuts, a richly browned bird (opposite) is a commanding showpiece and is nicely complemented by versions of traditional side dishes, like chestnut and apple dressing and a wild mountain cranberry sauce (above), as well as your favorite mashed potatoes and green vegetables. To retain the pure, sweet flavor of butternut squash, the soup (left) that starts the meal is cooked in water and cream instead of stock. Turn to pages 107–109 for recipes.*

WARM AND HEARTY WINTER SOUPS

SOUP TUREENS *Symbols of bounty and hospitality, soup tureens can do more than keep their contents warm. Ever since these portly vessels came into their own, particularly in the France of Louis XIV, they have always been something of a centerpiece standby. Whether on a dinner table, a mantel, or a sideboard, empty and lidded or filled with flowers, a tureen can be one of the loveliest focal points in any kitchen or dining room. At Christmas, expand the possibilities. Pile a tureen and several smaller bowls with mounds of glass balls. Or fill one with oranges and pinecones for the kitchen table. Arrange handfuls of Christmas crackers or little wrapped gifts in another, ready to be emptied by children's hands on Christmas morning.*

Made with exquisite ingredients—and served with a salad and crusty bread, of course—soup can be the central attraction of casual holiday entertaining. These four vibrant varieties combine homey goodness with regional and international traditions. Apples and chestnuts embrace in a velvety pureed soup (top left), rich with cream. Ginger and sherry perk up a Chinese corn and crab soup (top right), thick with crabmeat and crunchy water chestnuts. Carrots, orange juice, and ginger blend in a pureed soup (bottom left) that makes an ideal first course. Beets are the essence of our bracing borscht (bottom right), and lean chunks of short ribs add a satisfying complexity. Turn to pages 110–113 for the recipes.

SHEPHERD'S PIE *Made with slivers of sirloin braised in Cabernet Sauvignon, a savory shepherd's pie (left) is anything but humble. In this gratifying adaptation of a cozy pub classic, thin slices of carrots, onions, mushrooms, and leeks are simmered with the meat and wine, then spooned into individual baking dishes. To create a swirly crust, a mixture of mashed potatoes, sour cream, and butter is piped over the meat using a pastry bag. The pie is ready to serve, bubbling in its baking dish, when the potatoes start to brown. For the recipe, turn to page 114.*

TURKEY POT PIES *This elegant version of an old favorite (opposite) has a flaky cream-cheese pastry crowning a stew of root vegetables and turkey cooked in white wine. The maple-leaf-shaped crust is only one possibility; the dough can be cut into any shape that is large enough to cover the dish. The recipe is on page 116.*

CLAM CHOWDER IN A PASTRY DOME *Steamy under a dome of puff pastry, New England clam chowder (right) is an entire meal in a cup. In addition to keeping the soup warm, the crust takes the place of bread. Fresh clams, smoked bacon, and potatoes harmonize with heavy cream and white wine in the soup. Minus the topping, the chowder can be made in quantity ahead of time—and tastes even better the second day. For the recipe, turn to page 115.*

ICED CHOCOLATE MOUSSE

Shouldn't a Christmas gift be as rich as possible? Especially if it's dessert? Based on a classic, this airy mix of bittersweet chocolate, butter, and cream (right) is chilled for at least twelve hours. Make a show of it: Spoon the gooey indulgence into individual serving plates right at the table, and top each dollop with a little whipped cream, if you like. For the recipe, turn to page 117.

CHOCOLATE-BANANA-GINGER CAKE

With their wonderfully complementary flavors and textures, chocolate and almost any fruit are natural companions for dessert. In our elegant version of a timeless upside-down cake (left), a sumptuous chocolate batter, infused with fresh ginger, is baked atop a layer of sliced bananas. The recipe is on page 117.

POACHED PEARS, PAIRED

With necks as graceful as swans, pears are so sculptural that they're a natural for a centerpiece. They're also a tasty dessert, and even more so if they're transformed through the simple magic of wine and spices into our two poached desserts (right): raspberry-glazed pears in port wine syrup and poached pears in vanilla syrup. With a scoop of ice cream or whipped cream, these jewel-like treats make a refreshing finale to any holiday feast. The two recipes are on page 118.

CHAPTER SEVEN

Gifts from the Kitchen

* holiday spice cookies

* lemon butter cookies

* chocolate truffles

* homemade panettone

* rosemary-flavored vinegar

* classic winter pies

* gift basket ideas

* spicy nut gifts

FOOD IS PROBABLY THE MOST TRADITIONAL AND oldest holiday gift, an offering of bounty and nourishment during the year's bleakest season. From the rich breakfast the March sisters and their Marmee shared with hungry neighbors to the plump turkey devoured by a grateful Crachit family, food reminds us that Christmas was about feasting long before it was about shopping.

No gift you make yourself is ever insignificant. Wrapped in a cellophane bag, even a single cookie can delight a friend. The enjoyment begins as you pore over recipes, sampling flavors in your mind and anticipating the aromas that will fill your kitchen. There are treats for everyone,

Icing and shiny silver dragées make each holiday cookie, no matter the shape, as individual as a snowflake; cellophane sleeves keep the little gifts on view.

whether they are the whimsically iced butter cookies your colleagues wait for all year or the decadent pecan pie you bring to a neighbor's Boxing Day party. Savories such as herb-scented olives and fruity chutneys will please those friends who don't care for sweets. And if your gifts must travel, consider sturdy bar cookies or seasoned nuts that will arrive looking as perfect as they did when they left your kitchen.

As with any food, presentation is what transforms a sweet into an extra-thoughtful gift. Pile sugared almonds into a pair of Champagne flutes and nestle them in an excelsior-filled basket; stack a handful of *marrons glacés*, those classic French candied chestnuts, into a big café au lait bowl—the containers will be handy long after their contents have been eaten. Pair a lasting gift with a scrumptuous one by delivering a cake in the handsome pan in which you baked it. The many-layered Christmas trifle you carry to a party is hardly a trifle when it's presented in an exquisite glass bowl meant to be kept by your host. So be creative and wrap your food gifts to look as good as they taste.

A CAST OF COOKIES *What would the holidays be without cookies in many happy shapes? Sturdy Shaker boxes (opposite) protect their delicious contents and keep them a surprise until each lid is lifted. A lighthearted menagerie (above left) was created with contemporary and vintage cutters from* Victoria *editor Peggy Kennedy's remarkable collection. Packed closely in a parchment-lined box (left), a flurry of lemon butter snowflakes makes a heavenly gift. Turn to pages 119 and 120 for cookie recipes.*

COOKIES ON DISPLAY *Creatures as enchanting as these pose a question that's full of possibilities: Should they be devoured or admired? Brimming with crisp little cookies ready to be plucked for a snack, glass jars and vases (this page) make playful embellishments for a sideboard, mantel, or windowsill. Perhaps this is the year to create personalized cookies for your friends in shapes that represent their pets, their house, or their new baby. Decorations can be as simple as an outline of icing or a pair of raisin eyes.*

ORANGE-SCENTED MOCHA TRUFFLES *A gift of velvety homemade truffles is always welcome, particularly at a dinner party or an open house. Surprisingly easy to make, the creamy, melt-in-your-mouth morsels (opposite) get their delicate hint of orange from a splash of Grand Marnier or Cointreau. Instead of using a candy box, present them in a shallow, lidded basket lined with paper. Turn to page 121 for the recipe.*

Johnny-jump-up

BAMBOO CADDY *A clever gift carrier for cookies, candies, or small tarts, a bamboo dim-sum steamer (right) travels easily to any party. Take full advantage of the two layers by filling each one with a different delicacy. Remember to add an elegant ribbon. Later, the steamer can hold sewing notions or desk supplies—or perhaps it will remain in the kitchen, happily steaming away.*

BOXED PIES *Much prettier—and much longer lasting— than a cardboard bakery carton, a woven reed box dresses up every delivery on your holiday pie route. Before putting the lid on a maple pecan pie or lattice-topped cranberry apple pie (opposite), tuck in a copy of the recipe— see pages 122 and 123—for your friend. Write it on a lovely card or print it from your computer on a sheet of stationery.*

CHOCOLATE-CHIP PUMPKIN BREAD *Just because gift baskets are an old holiday tradition doesn't mean that their contents can't be a surprise. A French linen towel conceals a round of moist pumpkin bread (left) before it is given. The recipe is on page 124.*

FIGGY PUDDING *Steamed pudding (opposite, top row) is a Christmas classic; cinch it with a satin cord and a berry sprig or simply leave it in the silvery mold in which it was baked and tie the lid with a flouncy bow. The recipe is on page 125.*

PANETTONE *With its dried fruits and rum, this version of the Northern Italian holiday treat (opposite, bottom row) is baked in coffee cans. Wrap each can with brown paper and add a ribbon sash. Unmolded from the container, the tempting bread stands tall. Turn to page 126 for the recipe.*

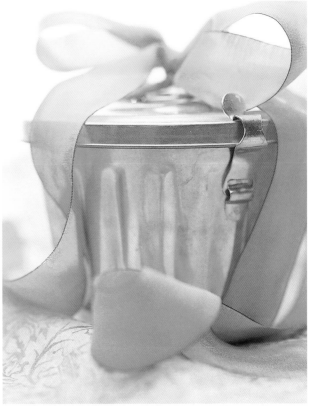

LINEN-WRAPPED OLIVES *Once in holiday finery, fragrant olives from the gourmet store make a savory bundle. Fill a vintage bowl with olives (left), tightly cover its top with plastic wrap to prevent a spill, and center it on a square of inexpensive linen, cut with pinking shears to keep the edges from unraveling. Gather the cloth, tie it with string, and add a sprig of greenery. Later, the linen can become a lining for a tray or a casual mat for drinks or candlesticks.*

LITTLE SNACK GIFT PACKS
Many store-bought cheese straws are so irresistible that they inspire a little enhancing. For incurable snackers on your list, turn the treats into stylish gifts (opposite). Stand them in flea-market jars tied with tags, slip several into a waxed paper bag, or wrap them in butcher paper and red twine.

CHRISTMAS TIN TRIOS *What's better than receiving a cheerfully familiar cookie tin of goodies? Receiving three! Many tins come in graduated sets of three (right), so be bold and fill them all. To make a generous gift—perfect for a weekend host—pack one tin with assorted crackers, one with a wheel of cheese, and another with nuts, perhaps one of the spicy preparations shown on pages 98 and 99. Or layer each with a complementary sweet—try gingersnaps, brownies, and caramels. Tie the tins together in a tower with a length of wide ribbon, as you would bundle a box around all four sides. You might also tie a star-tasseled cord around one of the lids, as we did. Either way, the gift is pretty enough to earn a place on the dessert pedestal.*

Merry
Christmas

To_____
From_____

"A Loin of mutton, Some Sugar, Butter and Bread, and 2 Pumpkin Pies." In 1808, Martha Ballard, a Maine midwife, recorded in her diary the gifts presented to her grown children, adding, "O happy has this year began and So may it proceed. . . ." It's tempting to picture Mrs. Ballard at the table, gingerly removing each cloth-covered container from a large hamper. Since it rarely holds just one item, a gift basket is the height of generosity. And long after its contents are gone, the basket remains.

❖ For gifts of homemade jams, dessert sauces, or chutneys (opposite), line shallow baskets or trays with vintage napkins and group similarly sized jars. To dress a jar, cover its lid with a square of fabric or paper cut with pinking shears and tie a ribbon to hold it in place. See page 127 for the cranberry pear chutney recipe.

❖ Gift baskets need not be made of wicker. Peanut butter and jelly, packed in vintage-style refrigerator containers (below), and a tea-towel-wrapped loaf of bread will amuse anyone with young children—or anyone who feels like a child. Tie the containers closed with string, slip in a wooden spreader, and add a manila tag stamped with the title of the gift.

❖ The pleasure of a gift basket, for giver as well as receiver, is multiplied by the number and kinds of items that go into the container. A bottle of wine and two stem glasses is a great beginning; once an antique corkscrew, tasting cup, decanter, and pair of crisp napkins have been added, the gift becomes an especially thoughtful gesture.

FLAVORED VINEGARS *Is there any kitchen habitué who wouldn't find a dozen uses for a gift of flavored vinegar? Rosemary and raspberry vinegars (left) are easy to make; they can even be concocted at summer harvest, months before the holiday chaos begins. Bottled for gift-giving in unusual glass flasks, flea-market cruets, or etched carafes, the vinegars look good on countertops and dinner tables alike. Both recipes appear on page 128.*

HERB-SPICED NUTS *What would the holidays be without nuts? They're essential in fruitcakes and in so many traditional cookies and candies. And a bowl of them in their shells virtually announces winter's arrival. Add an assortment of herb-spiced nuts to your repertoire, and bring a beautiful jarful the next time you attend one of those festive holiday cocktail parties. Turn to page 129 for the recipe.*

SHERRY AND ALMONDS GIFT *There aren't many gifts you can bring to an intimate winter gathering that are as elegantly golden as a bowl of spiced almonds (right) and their perfect match, a bottle of sherry. Whether a light, dry fino or a lush oloroso, sherry is enhanced by these distinctive nuts, which have been roasted in sugar, cumin, and smoked paprika. The recipe for the nuts is on page 129.*

Recipes

The recipes in this section appear in the same order in which the corresponding photographs appear in the chapters of this book. Below, for easy reference, they are listed alphabetically. The page number for the recipe is given first; the page number for the photograph is given second, in italics.

❖ herb-roasted fillet of beef ❖

YIELD: 8 TO 10 SERVINGS

4 tablespoons olive oil

3 tablespoons balsamic vinegar, or to taste

3 tablespoons minced fresh thyme,
　　or 3 teaspoons dried, crumbled

3 tablespoons minced fresh rosemary,
　　or 3 teaspoons dried, crumbled

1 tablespoon finely minced garlic

1 teaspoon coarsely ground black pepper,
　　or to taste

One 4- to 4½-pound trimmed fillet of beef,
　　patted dry and tied with kitchen string

2 teaspoons sea salt or coarse salt, or to taste

Fresh herb sprigs, for garnish

Horseradish Sauce (recipe follows)

The most succulent of beef cuts, a fillet is an appropriate extravagance at Christmas. In this version, the meat is flavored with a balsamic-infused rub, roasted in a hot oven, and garnished with herbs. In lieu of gravy, the fillet is accompanied by a snappy horseradish sauce.

1. In a small bowl, combine the olive oil, vinegar, thyme, rosemary, garlic, and black pepper. Rub the fillet with the mixture and wrap it in plastic wrap. Chill for 2 hours, or overnight.

2. Preheat the oven to 500°F.

3. Place the fillet on a rack in a roasting pan and sprinkle with the sea salt. Roast the fillet for 35 to 40 minutes, or until a meat thermometer inserted into the thickest part registers 130°F to 135°F for medium-rare meat. Transfer the fillet to a cutting board and let it cool, loosely covered, for 15 minutes.

4. Remove the strings from the meat. Cut the meat into thin slices and transfer the slices to a serving platter. Garnish with fresh herb sprigs and serve with Horseradish Sauce.

❖ horseradish sauce ❖

YIELD: ABOUT 2 CUPS

2 cups sour cream

½ cup peeled grated fresh horseradish
　　or drained bottled horseradish

2 tablespoons white wine vinegar

1 tablespoon freshly squeezed lemon juice

1 tablespoon Dijon mustard

1 teaspoon finely minced garlic

½ teaspoon sugar

Salt to taste

This creamy horseradish sauce works equally well with roasted lamb and, for a simple snack, burgers and fries. It can be made up to a day ahead and stored in the refrigerator.

1. Place a sieve lined with a double thickness of rinsed and squeezed-dry cheesecloth over a bowl, and add the sour cream. Let the sour cream drain in the refrigerator for 15 minutes. Discard the drained liquid, keeping the sour cream that remains in the sieve.

2. Transfer this sour cream to a bowl and whisk in the remaining ingredients. Transfer to a serving bowl, cover, and chill until ready to serve.

❖ w i l d - r i c e s a l a d ❖

YIELD: 8 TO 10 SERVINGS

4 cups cooked white rice

4 cups cooked wild rice

1 cup toasted pecan halves,
    broken into large pieces

1 cup dried cranberries or cherries, soaked in
    hot water for 10 minutes and drained

1 cup minced scallion

1/2 cup finely diced celery or fennel

1 red bell pepper, cored, seeded, and cut into
    small dice

1/3 cup minced parsley

1/4 cup snipped chives, dill, or tarragon,
    or a combination

FOR THE DRESSING

4 tablespoons rice vinegar or white wine
    vinegar

4 tablespoons freshly squeezed lemon juice

1 large garlic clove, minced and mashed
    to a paste

Salt and freshly ground black pepper to taste

1/3 to 1/2 cup canola oil or other vegetable oil,
    or to taste

2 to 3 tablespoons Asian sesame oil,
    or to taste

Hearty wild rice is a nostalgic side dish during the holidays, reminding us that the grain is an enduring tradition during winter months. For Christmas, pecans, cranberries, and red bell pepper add color and texture. Consider this a staple for brunch, buffet, or late-night supper. The salad can be made up to a day ahead and kept refrigerated. Serve it at room temperature for the most intense flavor.

1. In a large bowl, combine the rices, pecans, cranberries, scallion, celery, bell pepper, parsley, and chives. Mix to distribute the ingredients evenly.

2. Cover the salad and chill until ready to serve.

3. Make the dressing: In a bowl, whisk together the vinegar, lemon juice, garlic, and salt and pepper. Add the oils in a stream, whisking continuously, until the ingredients are well mixed. Just before serving, pour the dressing over the salad and toss to combine.

❖ f l a k y   c r e a m   b i s c u i t s ❖

YIELD: ABOUT 12 BISCUITS

2 cups flour

1 tablespoon baking powder

1 teaspoon salt

4 tablespoons cold unsalted butter,
    cut into bits

1 cup heavy cream

2 tablespoons unsalted butter, melted

How can something so humble be such a luxury? Our delicate biscuits are quickly put together with cold butter and cream, and bake in only 15 minutes. They are perhaps the ultimate holiday comfort food, elevating any meal to a home-and-hearth feast.

1. Preheat the oven to 425°F. Lightly grease a baking sheet.

2. Into a bowl, sift the flour, baking powder, and salt. Add the butter and blend with a pastry blender or two knives until the mixture resembles coarse meal.

3. Make a well in the center of the flour and add the cream. Stir the flour into the cream just until a dough is formed.

4. Transfer the dough to a lightly floured surface and knead gently for 1 minute. Pat out the dough to a $1/2$-inch thickness and stamp out rounds using a 2-inch round cookie cutter dipped in flour. Gather any remaining scraps, pat out, and form into rounds in the same manner.

5. Transfer the biscuits to the prepared baking sheet. Brush the tops and sides with the melted butter. Bake for 12 to 15 minutes, or until the biscuits are golden brown. Serve warm.

❖ s p i n a c h   a n d   f o n t i n a   c h e e s e   t a r t ❖

FOR THE TART SHELL

1½ cups all-purpose flour

½ teaspoon salt

6 tablespoons cold unsalted butter,
    cut into bits

2 tablespoons cold vegetable shortening

3 to 4 tablespoons ice water

FOR THE FILLING

3 tablespoons unsalted butter

⅓ cup minced shallots

1 cup finely diced shiitake or white
    mushrooms

One 10-ounce package frozen leaf spinach,
    cooked according to package directions,
    drained, patted dry, and chopped

2 teaspoons minced garlic

Salt and freshly ground black pepper to taste

3 large eggs

1 cup half-and-half

1½ cups freshly grated Italian Fontina cheese

¼ cup freshly grated Parmesan

Freshly grated nutmeg to taste

3 tablespoons fresh breadcrumbs

With its roots in the Mediterranean, this handsome spinach and cheese tart serves the holiday season well. Present it at dinner as a first course, or at lunch as a vegetarian main dish. It can be made earlier in the day; once it comes out of the oven, allow it to cool before refrigerating. It's best, though, at room temperature.

1. Make the tart shell: Into a bowl, sift the flour and salt. Add the butter and vegetable shortening. With a pastry blender or two knives, combine the mixture until it resembles coarse crumbs. Add enough ice water to gather the dough together in a ball. Knead the dough lightly and chill, wrapped in plastic wrap, for 30 minutes.

2. Preheat the oven to 400°F. On a lightly floured surface, roll out the dough to a ⅛-inch thickness and fit it into a 10-inch tart pan. Prick the bottom of the shell with a fork, line it with foil, and weight the foil with dried beans or raw rice. Bake the shell for 10 minutes. Remove the weights and foil and bake for 10 minutes more. Cool the shell in the pan on a rack.

3. Make the filling: In a skillet set over moderate heat, melt 2 tablespoons of the butter. Add the shallots and cook, stirring, for 2 to 3 minutes, or until the shallots have softened. Add the mushrooms and cook, stirring occasionally, for 4 minutes, or until the mushrooms are firm. Add the spinach, garlic, and salt and pepper, and cook the mixture, stirring, for 2 minutes more. Transfer the mixture to a bowl and let cool. Reduce the oven to 375°F.

4. In another bowl, whisk together the eggs and half-and-half. Whisk in the Fontina, 2 tablespoons of the Parmesan, and the nutmeg. Combine the egg mixture with the spinach mixture. Pour the filling into the shell. Sprinkle breadcrumbs and the remaining Parmesan over the filling and dot with the remaining tablespoon of butter. Bake the tart on a baking sheet for 25 to 30 minutes, or until set.

❖ o l d - f a s h i o n e d   l e m o n   b a r s ❖

YIELD: ABOUT 24 BARS

FOR THE SHORTBREAD BASE

2 sticks (1 cup) unsalted butter, softened

1/2 cup sugar, preferably superfine

1 teaspoon pure vanilla extract

2 1/2 cups all-purpose flour, sifted

FOR THE LEMON CURD

8 egg yolks

1 1/4 to 1 1/2 cups sugar

6 ounces freshly squeezed lemon juice

1 stick (1/2 cup) unsalted butter,
cut into tablespoons

1 1/2 tablespoons grated lemon peel

Confectioners' sugar, for garnish

Here is an example of two divine foods—shortbread and lemon curd—that combine to create a dessert that is greater than the sum of its parts. Both share a holiday tradition: Shortbread has long been a Christmas favorite, and citrus is a treasured part of the winter feast. You might want to make extra batches of both. With the shortbread, the second one can be dressed fresh from the oven with warm, strained raspberry preserves. Lemon curd, of course, is that rare food that can be enjoyed at any time of the day. Poured into a glass jar and handsomely labeled, it is a gift of sunshine.

1. Make the shortbread base: Generously butter a 13-by-9-by-2-inch baking pan. In the bowl of an electric mixer on medium speed, cream the butter until light and fluffy. Add the sugar a little at a time, beating until it is combined with the butter. Beat in the vanilla. Stir in the flour a little at a time until a dough is formed. Transfer the dough to the prepared baking pan and pat it into an even layer, making sure the edges are the same thickness as the center. Prick the dough with a fork and chill for 30 minutes.

2. Preheat the oven to 325°F. Bake the shortbread base for 40 to 45 minutes, or until it is a pale golden color. Transfer the pan to a rack to cool. Lower the oven temperature to 300°F.

3. Meanwhile, make the lemon curd: In a heavy saucepan, whisk together the yolks, sugar, lemon juice, and butter. Cook the mixture over medium-low heat, stirring with a wooden spoon, until it has thickened, about 5 minutes. Strain the curd into a bowl and stir in the grated lemon peel. Let the mixture cool 5 minutes.

4. Pour the curd over the shortbread base, smoothing it into an even layer, and bake for 10 minutes. Cool the pastry to room temperature and chill, covered with plastic wrap or foil (do not let the plastic or foil touch the curd), for 2 hours or overnight. Before serving, generously sift confectioners' sugar over the curd and cut into diamonds or squares. Serve bars at room temperature.

❖ a p r i c o t   n u t   c a k e ❖

YIELD: 8 TO 10 SERVINGS

2½ cups (about 1 pound) diced dried apricots

¼ cup diced candied orange peel

3 tablespoons orange-flavored liqueur
   or dark rum (if desired, substitute
   3 tablespoons orange juice)

2 cups all-purpose flour

2 teaspoons baking powder

1 teaspoon cinnamon

½ teaspoon freshly grated nutmeg

¼ teaspoon salt

1½ sticks (¾ cup) unsalted butter, softened

1 cup sugar

3 large eggs, lightly beaten

1 tablespoon grated orange peel

½ cup freshly squeezed orange juice

1 teaspoon pure vanilla extract

1 cup chopped toasted nuts such as pecans,
   hazelnuts, or walnuts

Confectioners' sugar, for dusting

Whole dried apricots, for garnish (optional)

Whole shelled nuts, for garnish (optional)

Eggnog Sauce (optional; recipe on the
   following page)

If you enjoy the custom of serving fruitcake at Christmas, consider this light, apricot-studded nut cake. We've scented the cake with cinnamon and nutmeg and dressed it in a dusting of confectioners' sugar, but, more deliciously, we've created a tangy eggnog sauce to serve with the slices. The cake can be prepared up to one week in advance; wrap it in plastic wrap and foil and store in a cool place.

1. Preheat the oven to 325°F. Butter and flour an 8-inch fluted tube or Bundt pan.

2. In a bowl, toss together the apricots, orange peel, and liqueur.

3. Into another bowl, sift the flour, baking powder, cinnamon, nutmeg, and salt.

4. In the bowl of an electric mixer set on medium speed, cream the butter. Add the sugar a little at a time and beat until the mixture is light and fluffy. Beat in the eggs a little at a time until the mixture is smooth. Beat in the orange peel.

5. In a small bowl, stir together the orange juice and the vanilla.

6. Add the flour mixture to the butter mixture a little at a time, alternating with the orange juice in increments and finishing with the flour. Fold in the fruit mixture and the nuts until just combined.

7. Transfer the batter to the pan, smoothing the top, and bake for 1¼ to 1½ hours, or until a cake tester inserted in the center comes out clean. Transfer the pan to a rack and let cool for 20 minutes. Invert the cake onto the rack and let cool completely.

8. Before serving, sift confectioners' sugar over the cake. If desired, garnish serving plate with apricots and nuts. With a serrated knife, cleaned in hot water frequently to prevent sticking, cut the cake into thin slices and serve with Eggnog Sauce or ice cream.

❖ e g g n o g s a u c e ❖

YIELD: ABOUT 2½ CUPS

2 cups half-and-half, scalded

⅓ cup sugar, or to taste

4 egg yolks

1 teaspoon pure vanilla extract

2 to 3 tablespoons bourbon

Freshly grated nutmeg to taste

Here is a versatile, rich eggnog sauce for holiday desserts. We like it with Apricot Nut Cake (recipe on previous page), and also with bread puddings, fruit pies, and Christmas trifles. The sauce's heady flavor is best when it's freshly made; grate the nutmeg just before serving.

1. In a saucepan, combine the hot half-and-half and the sugar, stirring until the sugar dissolves. In a bowl, whisk the egg yolks until combined. Add the half-and-half mixture in a stream, whisking until blended. Return the mixture to the saucepan. Cook over medium-low heat, stirring, until the sauce is thick enough to coat the back of a wooden spoon. Do not allow the mixture to boil or the sauce will curdle.

2. Strain the sauce into a bowl and stir in the vanilla and the bourbon. Let the sauce cool, then chill, covered, for 2 hours or overnight. Before serving, transfer the sauce to a sauceboat or serving bowl and sprinkle with freshly grated nutmeg.

❖ velouté of butternut squash soup ❖

YIELD: 6 TO 8 SERVINGS

10 tablespoons unsalted butter

2 medium butternut squash, peeled, seeded, and cubed

5 shallots, sliced

3 cloves garlic, minced

Salt and freshly ground black pepper to taste

1 bay leaf

1½ cups heavy cream

⅓ cup ground hazelnuts, toasted

Velouté: The very name conjures up smooth, warming sensations. Here the velouté is a rich soup of butternut squash, gently cooked in a bath of butter flavored with shallots and garlic. It's graced with heavy cream, lightly beaten, and a sprinkling of ground hazelnuts. Serve it with bread and a glass of wine for lunch or supper, or by itself as one elegant course of a grand dinner.

1. In a large saucepan or casserole, melt 6 tablespoons of butter over medium heat. Add the squash, shallots, garlic, salt and pepper, and the bay leaf, and continue to cook, stirring occasionally, for 5 minutes. Stir in ½ cup of the heavy cream and enough water to cover the vegetables by 1 inch, then bring to a boil. Reduce the heat and simmer, stirring occasionally, for 25 to 30 minutes, or until the squash is very tender. Remove and discard the bay leaf.

2. Transfer the mixture to a large bowl. In a food processor or blender, puree the mixture in batches and return it to the saucepan. If the mixture is too thick, thin with a little water or more cream. Bring the soup to a boil and simmer until heated through. Adjust the seasoning to taste.

3. In the bowl of an electric mixer set on medium-high speed, beat the remaining 1 cup of heavy cream until it is lightly thickened, to about the consistency of crème fraîche.

4. Ladle the soup into individual bowls and garnish each with a dollop of cream. Sprinkle each serving with ground hazelnuts.

❖ wild mountain cranberries ❖

5 ounces dry red wine such as Merlot
    or Cabernet Sauvignon

1²/₃ cups sugar

2 pounds wild mountain or cultivated
    cranberries

Peel and juice from 1/2 lemon

Peel and juice from 1/2 orange

A cheesecloth bag containing 1/2 cinnamon
    stick, 2 bay leaves, 15 peppercorns,
    3 star anise, and 10 juniper berries

Cranberry sauce, cranberry bread: The enjoyment of this tart fruit need not be limited to traditional favorites. Besides being a flavorful addition to salads, rice dishes, and stuffings, cranberries are divine as the stars of a recipe, all on their own. When cooking with wine, always choose a vintage you would enjoy by itself; good wine enhances any recipe in which it's included, while a poor one will not. Serve these cranberries as a side dish or as a garnish with turkey, ham, or pork.

In a saucepan, bring the wine and the sugar to a boil over medium heat, stirring, until the sugar dissolves. Add the remaining ingredients and the cheesecloth bag. Return the mixture to a boil, stirring frequently. Remove the pan from the heat. Transfer the cranberry mixture to a bowl and discard the cheesecloth bag. Let the cranberries cool, then chill, covered, for up to a week before serving.

❖ t r a d i t i o n a l   t u r k e y ❖
w i t h   c h e s t n u t   a n d   a p p l e   d r e s s i n g

YIELD: 6 TO 8 SERVINGS

One 14- to 16-pound fresh turkey

1/2 pound unsalted butter, softened

1 onion, diced

1/2 pound celery, sliced

1/2 pound fresh pork sausage

2 Granny Smith apples, peeled, cored,
    and diced

1 pound fresh chestnuts, roasted, peeled,
    and diced

4 cloves garlic, minced

Salt and freshly ground black pepper to taste

6 cups dried bread cubes

2 tablespoons minced fresh sage

1/3 cup minced fresh parsley

1 tablespoon minced fresh thyme

There really isn't any mystery to preparing a golden, succulent, tender turkey with tasty dressing. Begin with a fresh bird, not one that has been frozen; make bread cubes from a good-quality loaf, and choose only fresh herbs. Starting in a hot 400°F oven seals in the turkey's juices. When the temperature is lowered, the bird slowly roasts until perfectly done. To serve this masterpiece, garnish it lavishly with the foods of your choice. We would select lady apples and roasted unshelled chestnuts.

1. Preheat the oven to 400°F.

2. Rinse the turkey well, inside and out; pat dry with paper towels.

3. Prepare the dressing: In a large skillet, melt half the butter. Add the onion and celery, and cook over moderate heat, stirring frequently, until the vegetables are softened. Add the sausage, breaking it into small pieces, and cook, stirring occasionally, until it is no longer pink. Add the apples, chestnuts, garlic, and salt and pepper, and cook, stirring, for 3 minutes. Transfer the mixture to a large bowl. Stir in the bread cubes, sage, parsley, thyme, and more salt and pepper.

4. Salt the cavities of the turkey and spoon the dressing into the neck and body cavities, making sure not to pack it too tightly. Transfer any remaining dressing to a buttered shallow baking dish. Truss the bird and set it on a rack in a roasting pan. Rub the outside of the turkey with the remaining butter and season with salt and pepper.

5. Roast the turkey, uncovered, for 30 to 45 minutes, or until it is lightly browned. Cover it loosely with foil and reduce the temperature to 350°F. Continue to roast it, basting frequently with the pan juices, for 2 1/2 to 3 hours, or until the juices run clear when the thigh is pricked. Transfer the turkey to a cutting board, cover loosely with foil, and let stand for at least 20 minutes. Bake the remaining dressing, covered with foil, for 20 minutes. Uncover and bake for 10 minutes more, or until heated through.

6. Transfer the turkey to a serving platter. Untruss it and lightly fluff the dressing with a fork before serving.

❖ c h e s t n u t a n d a p p l e s o u p ❖

YIELD: 6 SERVINGS

2 tablespoons unsalted butter

1 white onion, minced

1 large carrot, minced

1 pound shelled chestnuts

4 Granny Smith apples, peeled, cored,
    and diced

2 tablespoons minced fresh thyme or
    1½ teaspoons dried, crumbled

2 tablespoons light brown sugar

1 cinnamon stick

Salt and freshly ground black pepper to taste

2 cups heavy cream

1 tablespoon minced fresh sage

Fresh chestnuts are available for a limited time each year, which happily coincides with the holiday season. They are marvelously versatile and always delicious, whether they're bought smoky and roasted in a little paper sack from a New York City street vendor; served as marrons glacés, *the French candied chestnuts; made into fillings for cakes and pastries; or cast in the starring role in savory dishes like this creamy soup.*

1. In a large saucepan set over medium heat, melt the butter. Add the onion and carrot, and cook, stirring occasionally, for 3 minutes. Add the chestnuts and apples, and cook, stirring occasionally, for 5 minutes more. Add 4 cups of water, the thyme, the brown sugar, the cinnamon stick, and salt and pepper. Bring the soup to a boil and simmer, stirring occasionally, for 25 minutes. Remove and discard the cinnamon stick.

2. Transfer the soup to a large bowl. In a blender or food processor, puree the soup in batches and return to the saucepan. Stir in the heavy cream and sage and bring the soup to a boil. Simmer for 15 minutes more. Before serving, adjust the seasoning, adding more salt and freshly ground pepper to taste.

❖ c o r n a n d c r a b s o u p ❖

6 cups chicken stock or low-sodium
    canned chicken broth

1/2 cup sliced water chestnuts

One 16-ounce can cream-style corn

1 teaspoon grated fresh gingerroot

1/2 pound cooked crabmeat

3 tablespoons cornstarch

2 tablespoons dry sherry

2 large egg whites, lightly beaten

1 whole large scallion, trimmed and thinly
    sliced, including the green part

2 to 3 teaspoons sesame oil, or to taste

Salt to taste

Hectic days, social evenings, endless to-do lists—all are part of the wonder and joy of Christmas. But as busy as we are, we wouldn't trade these activities. Still, it helps to have a recipe like this one on hand, a corn and crab soup spiked with sherry and fresh ginger. One of its many virtues is that it can be prepared from foods generally kept on the pantry shelf, and in just a few minutes. The crab and sherry contribute a note of luxury, the chicken stock and corn one of comfort. Here is a sublime culinary contradiction: a practical, last-minute indulgence.

1. In a large saucepan, combine the chicken stock, water chestnuts, corn, and gingerroot. Bring the mixture to a boil, stirring occasionally, and simmer for 10 minutes. Stir in the crabmeat.

2. In a bowl, combine the cornstarch, 1/4 cup water, and the sherry. Stir until the mixture is smooth and lump-free. Add the cornstarch mixture to the simmering soup and stir until the soup thickens slightly. Remove from the heat. Add the egg whites to the hot soup in a stream, stirring, until threads are formed. Stir in the scallion, sesame oil, and salt. Transfer to a tureen or individual soup plates and serve.

❖ gingered orange-carrot soup ❖

3 tablespoons olive oil

1 pound carrots, peeled and sliced

1 onion, minced

1 tablespoon minced garlic

1 tablespoon minced fresh gingerroot

Salt and freshly ground pepper to taste

5 cups chicken stock or low-sodium canned
   chicken broth

2 teaspoons grated orange zest

1 bay leaf

½ cup freshly squeezed orange juice

Freshly squeezed lemon juice to taste

Sour cream or low-fat plain yogurt, for garnish

Minced fresh cilantro or parsley, for garnish

Dress them up, dress them down: Soups are the unsung heroes of holiday tables. Consider, though, trying some new combinations for this special season, such as a gingery orange and carrot soup. If you prefer, the chicken broth can be replaced with a good vegetable stock.

1. In a large saucepan set over medium heat, heat the olive oil. Add the carrots, onion, garlic, gingerroot, and salt and pepper. Cook, stirring occasionally, until the onion is golden, 7 to 8 minutes. Add the chicken stock, orange zest, and bay leaf, and bring to a boil. Reduce the heat and simmer, covered, stirring occasionally, for 30 minutes. Remove and discard the bay leaf.

2. Transfer the soup to a large bowl. In a food processor or blender, puree the soup in batches. Return it to the saucepan. Stir in the orange juice and season with salt and pepper and lemon juice. Simmer the soup until it has heated through. Ladle the soup into individual bowls or a tureen. Garnish each serving with sour cream and cilantro.

❖ b o r s c h t ❖

2 pounds beef short ribs, cut between the
    bones into large pieces

4 onions, 2 left whole and 2 thinly sliced

4 whole cloves

3 carrots, peeled and sliced

2 celery stalks, sliced

1 bay leaf

1 large sprig of fresh thyme or 1 teaspoon
    dried, crumbled

1/2 teaspoon peppercorns

Salt and freshly ground pepper to taste

2 pounds beets, unpeeled, with 1-inch tops
    left intact

2 tablespoons unsalted butter

1 tablespoon minced garlic

1 pound (4 cups) Savoy or green cabbage,
    shredded or grated

1 large potato, shredded or grated

1/2 cup sugar

2/3 to 1 cup red wine vinegar, or to taste

Sour cream, for garnish

Snipped fresh dill sprigs, for garnish

Serve borscht at holiday dinners, for its color alone. Yes, the flavor—complex with beef, aromatic vegetables, beets, cabbage, sugar, and red wine vinegar—is superb. But the color, a rich pinky red with a swirl of pristine sour cream, enchants and delights the eye. Serve it with pumpernickel or another dark, chewy bread.

1. In a large casserole or stockpot, combine the short ribs, 2 whole onions, each studded with 2 of the cloves, 1 of the sliced carrots, the celery, bay leaf, thyme, peppercorns, salt, and enough water to cover the ribs by 2 inches. Bring to a boil and simmer, skimming occasionally, for 2 hours. Transfer the ribs to a cutting board, remove the meat from the bones, discarding bones and any gristle or fat, and cut the meat into small pieces. Transfer the meat to a bowl and reserve. Strain the cooking liquid, bring it to a boil, and reduce to 6 cups.

2. Meanwhile, in a saucepan, combine the beets with enough water to cover them by 1 inch, add salt, and bring to a boil. Simmer covered, for 30 minutes, or until just tender. Drain the beets and let them cool enough to handle. Strain the cooking liquid through a fine sieve and reserve 3 1/2 cups. Peel the beets, cut them into julienne strips, and set aside.

3. In a casserole or large saucepan over medium heat, melt the butter, add the remaining sliced onions and salt, and cook, stirring occasionally, until the onions are golden. Add the garlic and remaining carrots and cook, stirring, for 1 minute. Add the cabbage, potato, reserved stock, and salt and pepper, bring to a boil, and simmer, skimming, for 20 minutes.

4. In a saucepan, heat the sugar with 1 tablespoon water until it is melted and golden. Remove the sugar water from the heat and add the vinegar. Return the saucepan to the heat and add 1/2 cup of reserved beet liquid and simmer the mixture, stirring, until the sugar dissolves.

5. To the cabbage mixture, add the reserved meat, beets, beet/vinegar liquid to taste, remaining beet cooking liquid, and salt and pepper. Simmer 20 minutes longer. Ladle the soup into bowls and garnish each serving with a dollop of sour cream and a sprinkle of dill.

❖ s h e p h e r d ' s   p i e ❖

YIELD: 6 SERVINGS

2 tablespoons vegetable oil

3 pounds sirloin, cut into thin slivers

2 white onions, diced

2 large carrots, thinly sliced

1 leek, white and pale green parts,
    thinly sliced

1 cup Cabernet Sauvignon

12 button mushrooms, trimmed, wiped clean,
    and sliced

1 tablespoon minced fresh thyme

1 tablespoon minced fresh parsley

1 teaspoon minced garlic

1 cup veal stock or beef broth

Salt and freshly ground pepper to taste

4 Idaho potatoes, peeled and cut into cubes

1 cup sour cream

1 tablespoon unsalted butter

The English have contributed so many of our Christmas customs, and shepherd's pie is a sterling example. A hearty mixture of beef, vegetables, and wine is simmered, then covered in a cloud of mashed potatoes—this is a crowd-pleaser indeed. In order to slice the beef into slivers, freeze it briefly to make it easier to handle.

1. In a large saucepan or casserole, heat the oil. Add the sirloin and cook over medium heat, stirring occasionally, until it has browned. Add the onions, carrots, and leek. Cook, stirring occasionally, for 5 minutes. Pour in the wine and simmer for 10 minutes. Add the mushrooms, thyme, parsley, and garlic, and continue to cook for 5 minutes more. Stir in the veal stock and bring to a boil. Simmer, stirring occasionally, for 30 minutes. Adjust the seasoning, adding salt and pepper.

2. Meanwhile, in a saucepan, combine the potatoes with water to cover by 2 inches and salt to taste. Bring to a boil and simmer, covered, for 20 to 25 minutes, or until the potatoes are tender when pierced with a fork. Drain the potatoes and put them through a ricer or food mill into a large bowl. Add the sour cream, butter, and salt and pepper, and stir until the mixture is smooth and well combined.

3. Preheat the oven to 350°F. Transfer the meat mixture to a shallow baking dish. Fit a large star tip into a pastry bag and spoon the potato mixture into the bag. Decoratively pipe the potatoes over the meat mixture until it is covered. Alternatively, you can spoon the potato mixture onto the meat. Bake for 30 minutes, or until the potatoes are golden.

❖ c l a m   c h o w d e r   i n   a   p a s t r y   d o m e ❖

YIELD: 6 SERVINGS

24 large fresh clams, scrubbed and rinsed well

2 cups dry white wine

2 tablespoons vegetable oil

1 large white onion, diced

1 leek, white and pale green parts, diced

2 stalks celery, diced

2 slices smoked bacon, diced

2 Idaho potatoes, peeled and diced

1 quart heavy cream

2 tablespoons minced fresh thyme

Salt and freshly ground pepper to taste

One 1-pound package frozen puff-pastry dough, thawed

1 large egg plus 1 large egg yolk

It's the holidays: Pull out all the stops. At least it will seem that you have when your guests spot these bowls with their spectacular domes of golden puff pastry and succulent, steamy clam chowder underneath. Frozen puff pastry should be a staple for every kitchen; buy the finest quality you can find, and it will be one of those foods that is just about as good as homemade. Considering how laborious it is to make puff pastry, it's worth the investment.

1. In a large saucepan or casserole, combine the clams and the wine. Cover the pan and bring the liquid to a boil. Steam the clams, shaking the pan occasionally, for 8 to 10 minutes, or until they have opened. Shuck the clams, reserving the juice, and strain the juice through a fine sieve into a bowl. Quarter each clam and transfer to a bowl.

2. In the saucepan set over medium heat, heat the oil. Add the onion, leek, celery, and bacon. Cover and cook the mixture, stirring occasionally, for 5 minutes. Stir in the reserved cooking liquid from the clams and simmer 10 minutes. Add the potatoes, cream, thyme, and salt and pepper. Bring the mixture to a boil and simmer, stirring occasionally, for 25 to 30 minutes, or until the potatoes are tender. Stir in the clams and adjust the seasoning, adding salt and pepper. Divide the hot soup among six ovenproof bowls.

3. Preheat the oven to 400°F.

4. Cut the puff pastry into circles that are large enough to cover each bowl. In a small bowl, combine the egg, egg yolk, 1 teaspoon water, and a pinch of salt, and mix well. Brush the edge of each pastry circle with the egg mixture and invert the circles onto the bowls, pressing the edges of the pastry onto the bowls to seal. Brush the tops of the pastry with the egg wash. Lightly score the pastry in a crosshatch design. Arrange the bowls on a baking sheet. Bake the soup for 10 to 12 minutes, or until the pastry is puffed and golden.

❖ turkey pot pies ❖
with cream-cheese crust

YIELD: 6 SERVINGS

FOR THE CREAM-CHEESE CRUST

1 pound all-purpose flour

1/2 teaspoon salt, or to taste

1 pound unsalted butter, cut into dice

1 pound softened cream cheese, cut into cubes

FOR THE TURKEY PIE

3 tablespoons vegetable oil

2 pounds fresh turkey legs and thighs

Salt and freshly ground pepper to taste

1 large onion, diced

1 quart low-sodium canned chicken broth

2 stalks celery, peeled and sliced

2 large carrots, diced

2 parsnips, diced

2 cups diced sweet potatoes

1 cup diced rutabaga

2 cups English peas, blanched,
   or frozen peas, thawed

1 tablespoon each chopped fresh oregano,
   marjoram, and parsley

1 tablespoon snipped fresh chives

1 large egg plus 1 large egg yolk

Christmas comfort food? You'll not find anything better than pot pie—pot pie that is rich with fresh turkey, sweet potatoes, and peas, all baked in a heavenly cream-cheese pastry crust.

1. Make the crust: In the bowl of an electric mixer fitted with the paddle attachment, combine the flour, salt, and butter, and mix on low until the mixture resembles coarse meal. Add the cream cheese and continue to mix until ingredients are combined; some streaks of cheese will remain. Shape the dough into two balls, flatten each ball into a disk, and wrap in plastic wrap. Chill for at least 1 hour, or until firm enough to roll.

2. If making individual pot pies, on a lightly floured surface roll out dough to a 1/4-inch thickness and cut into decorative shapes that are large enough to cover each dish. Wrap the shapes in plastic wrap and freeze until ready to bake. For one large pie, roll out the dough to a 1/4-inch-thick sheet large enough to cover the dish. Wrap in plastic and freeze.

3. In a casserole set over medium-high heat, heat the oil until hot. Add the turkey and the salt and pepper. Cook, turning occasionally, until the turkey is brown. Add the onion and cook the mixture, covered, over medium heat, stirring occasionally, for 5 minutes. Add the broth and simmer, uncovered, for 1 hour. Strain the liquid into a bowl and set aside. Cool the turkey and remove it from the bones; cut into large pieces.

4. In a casserole set over medium-high heat, combine the turkey, celery, carrots, parsnips, sweet potatoes, rutabaga, reserved stock, and salt and pepper to taste. Bring to a boil and simmer, stirring occasionally, for 30 minutes, or until the vegetables are tender. Stir in the peas and fresh herbs, and adjust the seasoning.

5. Preheat the oven to 350°F. In a small bowl, lightly beat the egg, egg yolk, 1 teaspoon water, and a pinch of salt. Transfer the filling to six individual ovenproof bowls or to one large shallow casserole and top with the frozen pastry. Brush the pastry with the egg wash and bake for 30 to 45 minutes, or until the crust is golden.

❖ i c e d c h o c o l a t e m o u s s e ❖

YIELD: 6 SERVINGS

1 cup heavy cream

8 ounces bittersweet chocolate, cut into pieces

6 tablespoons unsalted butter, cut into bits

1 teaspoon vanilla extract

4 large eggs, separated (see Note)

1/4 cup sugar

1. In a saucepan set over medium heat, scald the cream. Add the chocolate over medium-low heat a little at a time, stirring, until melted and smooth. Remove from the heat and stir in the butter a little at a time and add the vanilla. Whisk in the egg yolks, one at a time, until the mixture is combined well.

2. In the bowl of an electric mixer, beat the whites until they hold soft peaks. Add the sugar a little at a time and beat until whites hold firm peaks. Stir a quarter of the whites into the chocolate mixture and gently but thoroughly fold in the remaining whites in three additions.

3. Transfer the mixture to a serving dish and chill, covered, for 12 hours.

Note: There is a small health risk associated with using raw or lightly cooked eggs. Please use only properly refrigerated, clean, sound-shelled AA- or A-grade eggs.

❖ c h o c o l a t e - b a n a n a - g i n g e r c a k e ❖

YIELD: 6 SERVINGS

3 firm ripe bananas

1 cup all-purpose flour

4 tablespoons bittersweet cocoa powder

2 teaspoons baking powder

1 tablespoon grated fresh gingerroot

1 stick (1/2 cup) unsalted butter, softened

1 cup granulated sugar

2 large eggs, lightly beaten

Confectioners' sugar, for garnish

1. Preheat the oven to 350°F. Butter a 9-inch round cake or pie pan. Peel and cut the bananas into slices about 1/3 inch thick. Arrange the slices in one layer in the bottom of the prepared pan.

2. Into a bowl, sift the flour, cocoa, and baking powder. Stir in the ginger.

3. In the bowl of an electric mixer on medium speed, cream the butter with the granulated sugar until light and fluffy. Beat in the eggs, a little at a time, until well combined. Add the flour mixture to the egg mixture and mix until combined well.

4. Spoon the batter over the bananas, smoothing the top, and bake for 25 to 30 minutes, or until a cake tester inserted in the center comes out clean. Let cool in the pan for 10 minutes and invert onto a serving dish to cool completely. Sift confectioners' sugar over the cake before serving.

❖ poached pears in vanilla syrup ❖

YIELD: 4 SERVINGS

2 cups dry white wine

1½ cups sugar

1 lemon, juiced, and peel removed

1 vanilla bean, split lengthwise

1 cinnamon stick

4 medium, firm ripe pears such as Bosc,
  Bartlett, or Anjou

In a season of sweet snacks and rich meals, a dessert of poached pears is as refreshing as sorbet. Serve these with ice cream, if you wish.

1. In a saucepan large enough to hold the pears in one layer, combine 2 cups water, the wine, the sugar, and the lemon peel and juice. Add the vanilla bean and cinnamon stick. Stirring over moderate heat, bring to a boil.

2. Peel the pears, leaving the stems intact. Place the pears in the poaching liquid as they are peeled, arranged in one layer. The liquid should just cover the pears. If not, add water. Poach the pears at a bare simmer for 12 to 15 minutes, or until just tender. Let them cool in the pan.

3. With a slotted spoon, transfer pears to a bowl. Remove the vanilla bean and cinnamon. Over medium-high heat, reduce liquid until slightly thickened; let cool. Strain liquid over pears. Chill, covered, until ready to serve.

❖ raspberry-glazed pears ❖
in port wine syrup

YIELD: 4 SERVINGS

2 cups dry red wine

1 cup port wine

1½ cups sugar

4 strips orange peel

½ cup freshly squeezed orange juice

1 cinnamon stick

4 whole cloves or 1 star anise

4 medium, firm ripe pears such as Bosc,
  Bartlett, or Anjou

⅔ cup sieved raspberry preserves

Lightly whipped cream, for serving

1. In a saucepan large enough to hold the pears in one layer, combine 1 cup water with the red wine, port, sugar, orange peel, orange juice, cinnamon stick, and cloves. Bring the mixture to a boil over medium heat, stirring, then simmer until the sugar dissolves.

2. Peel the pears, leaving the stems intact, and add them to the syrup as they are peeled. Arrange the pears in one layer. The pears should be just covered by liquid; if not, add water. Poach the pears at a bare simmer for 12 to 15 minutes, or until just tender. Let them cool in the liquid, then transfer them to a serving dish with a slotted spoon. Heat the cooking liquid to boiling and reduce to 2 cups. Strain the liquid into another saucepan. Add the sieved raspberry preserves and simmer over moderate heat, stirring, until the mixture is thickened. Spoon the syrup over the pears. Serve with lightly whipped cream.

❖ h o l i d a y   s p i c e   c o o k i e s ❖

YIELD: 3 TO 4 DOZEN COOKIES,
DEPENDING ON THEIR SIZE

FOR THE COOKIES

1 cup (2 sticks) unsalted butter, softened

1 cup firmly packed light brown sugar

1 cup granulated sugar

2 large eggs

4 cups all-purpose flour

2 teaspoons baking powder

1 tablespoon cinnamon

1 teaspoon freshly grated nutmeg

1/2 teaspoon ground cloves

1/2 teaspoon salt

2 to 3 tablespoons heavy cream, as needed

FOR THE ICING

1 pound confectioners' sugar

2 large egg whites

Food coloring, if desired

Here is the most versatile, reliable Christmas cookie recipe ever. Make these into delicious treats to serve as dessert with ice cream; present them at a buffet or cookie party; or make them to decorate your home. They can be strung on the tree or hung from windows, mantels, and frames (for the ribbon attachment, create a hole in the cookie with a drinking straw before baking). With the icing, write messages on them for gift tags, place cards, even Christmas postcards. They can be stored in an airtight container for up to ten days.

1. In the bowl of an electric mixer set at medium speed, cream the butter, adding the sugars a little at a time, until the mixture is light and fluffy. Do not overbeat. Add the eggs one at a time, mixing well after each addition. Into a bowl, sift the flour, baking powder, cinnamon, nutmeg, cloves, and salt. Add the dry ingredients to the butter mixture and enough of the cream to form a dough. Divide the dough in half, shape each half into a ball, and transfer to a sheet of waxed paper. Pat each ball into a 1/2-inch-thick disk and wrap it in waxed paper. Chill for 2 hours.

2. Preheat the oven to 350°F. Line baking sheets with parchment paper. Let the chilled dough soften at room temperature for 5 to 10 minutes, until it can be rolled. Between sheets of lightly floured waxed paper, roll out the dough to a little more than 1/8 inch thick. With cookie cutters dipped in flour, cut out shapes and arrange 1 inch apart on the baking sheets. Bake for 7 to 8 minutes, or until firm to the touch. Cool the cookies on the sheets for 5 minutes and transfer to racks to cool completely.

3. Make the icing: In the bowl of an electric mixer set at low speed, combine the confectioners' sugar and egg whites. Beat until the sugar is completely moistened. Increase the speed to high and beat for 5 minutes, or until the icing forms stiff peaks. Tint the icing with food coloring, if desired.

4. Fit pastry bags with small, plain tips. Transfer the icing to the pastry bags. Decorate the cookies as desired.

❖ l e m o n   b u t t e r   c o o k i e s ❖

YIELD: 3 TO 4 DOZEN COOKIES,
DEPENDING ON THEIR SIZE

4 cups all-purpose flour

1 teaspoon baking powder

$1/4$ teaspoon baking soda

$1/2$ teaspoon salt

1 cup softened unsalted butter

2 cups sugar

2 large eggs, lightly beaten

2 tablespoons finely grated lemon peel

2 tablespoons freshly squeezed lemon juice

2 teaspoons pure vanilla extract

FOR THE ICING

1 pound confectioners' sugar

2 large egg whites

Food coloring, if desired

These tender, buttery cookies will enchant everyone. If you like to present guests with favors, consider making these as giant stars, snowflakes, and wreaths. Decorate them lavishly with icing and silver or gold dragées. Once the icing has set, slip each one into a cellophane or glassine envelope and tie it closed with a pretty ribbon. Attach a gift tag to each one, or arrange them on a silver tea tray.

1. Into a bowl, sift the flour, baking powder, baking soda, and salt. In the bowl of an electric mixer, cream the butter slightly. Add the sugar a little at a time, and beat the mixture until it is light and fluffy. Do not over-beat. Beat in the eggs a little at a time, mixing well after each addition. Beat in the lemon peel, lemon juice, and vanilla until the mixture comes together. Shape the dough into a ball; divide it in half and transfer to a sheet of waxed paper. Pat each half into a $1/2$-inch-thick disk and wrap it in waxed paper. Chill for 2 hours.

2. Preheat the oven to 350°F. Line baking sheets with parchment paper. Let the chilled dough soften at room temperature for 5 to 10 minutes, until it can be rolled. Roll out the dough between sheets of lightly floured waxed paper to $1/8$ inch thick. Cut out shapes with cookie cutters dipped in flour and arrange them 1 inch apart on the baking sheets. Bake for 7 to 8 minutes, or until the edges of the cookies are a pale golden color. Cool the cookies on the sheets for 5 minutes and transfer to racks to cool completely.

3. Make the icing: In the bowl of an electric mixer, combine the confectioners' sugar and egg whites and beat the mixture on low speed until the sugar is moistened. Increase the speed to high and beat for 5 minutes, or until the icing forms stiff peaks. Add food coloring, if desired.

4. Fit pastry bags with small, plain tips. Fill the bags with icing and decorate the cookies.

❖ orange-scented mocha truffles ❖

YIELD: ABOUT 2 DOZEN TRUFFLES

8 ounces bittersweet chocolate, coarsely
chopped

1/3 cup heavy cream

1 tablespoon freshly ground espresso powder

4 tablespoons unsalted butter

1 teaspoon grated orange peel

1 to 2 tablespoons Grand Marnier or
Cointreau

Sifted unsweetened Dutch-process
cocoa powder

Sifted confectioners' sugar

For sheer holiday extravagance, chocolate truffles reign supreme. They fetch quite a high price at the chocolaterie, but, happily, they are fairly simple to make in your own kitchen. Truffles are made from a mixture called ganache—an elegant combination of chocolate, heavy cream, and sweet butter. Here they are flavored with espresso and Grand Marnier, but you can also infuse them with other liqueurs, such as framboise or Cognac or amaretto. Similarly, you can roll the shaped truffles in finely chopped pistachios, walnuts, hazelnuts, or pecans, or in shredded coconut. One caveat: Never scrimp on chocolate! Buy the finest quality you can find. Because chocolate is so sensitive to temperature, it's best to shape the truffles in a cool room; an overheated kitchen with hot ovens and pots simmering on the stove will produce a slippery, melted mess. Once made, truffles can be stored in one layer in an airtight container in the refrigerator for up to ten days. Before serving, allow them to sit at room temperature for 20 to 30 minutes, when their flavor will be its most intense.

1. In the top of a double boiler set over but not touching simmering water, melt the chocolate. Remove the pan from the heat. In a small saucepan, scald the cream. Add the espresso powder and stir until it dissolves. Pour the cream mixture into the chocolate, stirring with a wooden spoon. Stir in the butter, orange peel, and Grand Marnier. Transfer the truffle mixture to a bowl, cover with plastic wrap, and chill for 1 hour, or until firm.

2. To shape the truffles, dust the palms of your hands with cocoa powder. Pinch off a heaping teaspoon of the mixture and roll it between your palms into a 1-inch ball. Continue with the remainder of the mixture. Dredge half the truffles in cocoa, shaking off the excess, and the other half in confectioners' sugar. Place each truffle in a fluted paper or foil candy cup.

❖ maple pecan pie ❖

YIELD: 1 PIE, 6 TO 8 SERVINGS

FOR THE PASTRY

1½ cups all-purpose flour

¼ teaspoon salt

1 stick (½ cup) cold unsalted butter,
   cut into bits

3 to 4 tablespoons ice water

FOR THE FILLING

1 pound pecan halves

½ cup maple syrup

½ cup dark corn syrup

⅓ cup sugar

4 ounces bittersweet chocolate, melted

4 tablespoons unsalted butter, melted

4 large eggs

2 tablespoons dark rum

1 large egg

Confectioners' sugar, for garnish

Pie could easily be our national dessert; make your pie with pecans, indigenous to the South, and you have the ultimate dessert. The sweetness of this pecan pie is balanced by bittersweet chocolate and rum.

1. Make the pastry: Into a bowl, sift the flour and salt. Add the butter and, with a pastry blender or two knives, blend the mixture until it resembles coarse meal. Stir in the water until the mixture forms a ball. Transfer the dough to a lightly floured surface and gently knead it until it is combined well. Flatten the dough into a disk, wrap in plastic wrap, and chill for 30 minutes.

2. Preheat the oven to 350°F. On a lightly floured surface, roll the dough into a round about ⅛ inch thick and fit it into a deep pie plate, fluting the edges. Gather the scraps of dough and roll them into a round ⅛ inch thick for cutting out leaf shapes. Prick the bottom of the crust and chill, together with the remaining dough, while preparing the filling.

3. Make the filling: Coarsely chop enough pecans to make 3 cups. Spread the pecans, including the remaining whole ones, on a baking sheet and bake for 5 to 7 minutes, stirring occasionally, until they are lightly toasted. Set aside to cool.

4. In a bowl, combine the maple syrup, corn syrup, sugar, chocolate, and butter. Whisk in the eggs, one at a time, and the rum. Stir in the chopped pecans. Pour the filling into the pie shell and arrange the remaining pecan halves in a decorative design on top. Bake the pie on a baking sheet in the lower third of the oven for 40 to 45 minutes, or until set.

5. While the pie is baking, make the pastry leaves. Roll out the remaining dough and cut it into leaf shapes. With the tip of a knife, score the leaves to simulate veins. Arrange them on an ungreased baking sheet.

6. In a small bowl, lightly beat the egg with 1 teaspoon water. Brush the pastry leaves with the egg wash and bake for 8 to 10 minutes. Let the pie and leaves cool on a rack to room temperature. Sift confectioners' sugar over the pie before serving and garnish with the pastry leaves.

❖ c r a n b e r r y   a p p l e   p i e ❖

YIELD: ONE PIE, 6 TO 8 SERVINGS

FOR THE PASTRY

2½ cups all-purpose flour

½ teaspoon salt

4 tablespoons cold unsalted butter,
    cut into bits

½ cup cold vegetable shortening

¼ cup ice water

FOR THE FILLING

1 cup dried cranberries

2½ pounds (about 6) Granny Smith apples

2 tablespoons freshly squeezed lemon juice

½ cup sugar, or to taste

3 tablespoons flour

1 teaspoon cinnamon

¼ teaspoon freshly grated nutmeg

¼ teaspoon ground ginger

¼ teaspoon salt

1 teaspoon grated lemon peel

2 tablespoons unsalted butter, cut into bits

1 large egg

The fruits of winter, especially tart cranberries and Granny Smith apples, are pie staples. Here they are colorful as well, peeking out from under their sweet lattice top.

1. Make the pastry: Into a bowl, sift the flour and salt. Add the butter and shortening and, with a pastry blender, combine until the mixture resembles coarse meal. Tossing with a fork, add enough ice water to make a soft but not sticky dough. Shape the dough into a ball. Divide the ball in half, dust with flour and chill, wrapped in plastic wrap, for 1 hour.

2. On a lightly floured surface, roll out half the dough to a round ⅛ inch thick; fit the dough into a deep pie plate. Leaving a 1-inch overhang, trim the excess dough. Prick the shell with a fork and chill for 30 minutes.

3. On a lightly floured surface, roll out the other ball of dough ⅛ inch thick. With a knife, cut the dough into ½-inch strips, 10 to 12 inches long. Transfer the strips to a baking sheet and chill for 10 minutes, or until just firm enough to handle. Preheat the oven to 425°F.

4. Make the filling: In a small saucepan, combine the cranberries with 1 cup water, bring to a simmer, and remove from the heat. Let stand 15 minutes and drain.

5. Peel, core, and thinly slice the apples. In a bowl, combine the apples, lemon juice, drained cranberries, sugar, flour, spices, salt, lemon peel, and butter. Pour the filling into the shell, spreading it evenly. Arrange the pastry strips in a lattice pattern over the apples. Trim the strips flush with the overhang of the shell, pressing them onto the shell. Turn up the dough and crimp the edge decoratively.

6. In a small bowl, beat the egg with 1 tablespoon water. Brush the pastry with the egg wash. Bake the pie on a baking sheet in the lower third of the oven for 15 minutes. Reduce the heat to 375°F and bake for 45 minutes, or until the filling bubbles. If the pie begins to brown too much, cover it loosely with foil. Transfer the pie to a rack to cool.

❖ c h o c o l a t e - c h i p   p u m p k i n   b r e a d ❖

YIELD: 1 BUNDT CAKE, 6 TO 8 SERVINGS

3 cups all-purpose flour

2 teaspoons baking powder

1/2 teaspoon salt

1 1/2 teaspoons cinnamon

1/2 teaspoon freshly grated nutmeg

1/4 teaspoon ground ginger

1/4 teaspoon ground cloves

10 tablespoons unsalted butter, softened

2/3 cup firmly packed light brown sugar

2/3 cup granulated sugar

2 large eggs, beaten lightly

1 teaspoon pure vanilla extract

One 15- to 16-ounce can pumpkin puree

1 cup chocolate chips

1 cup chopped walnuts or pecans

Confectioners' sugar, for garnish

For many, the holiday season is full of last-minute arrangements and impromptu guests. For many, too, gift lists seem to grow longer each year. For just these situations, our rich, tender pumpkin bread is an inspired choice. The bread can be stored, tightly wrapped, in the refrigerator for up to five days, so it is at hand whenever company calls. It's lovely with tea or a glass of sherry and makes a fine dessert after a casual supper. This is also a sturdy cake that can be packed in all manner of gift boxes to send to dear ones; on arrival, it will be as impeccable as it was when it left your kitchen. To make this gift even more memorable, transcribe the recipe and tuck it in alongside the cake.

1. Preheat the oven to 350°F. Butter and flour a 10-inch tube or Bundt pan.

2. Into a bowl, sift the flour, baking powder, salt, cinnamon, nutmeg, ginger, and cloves.

3. In the bowl of an electric mixer set at medium speed, cream the butter slightly. Add the light brown sugar and the granulated sugar a little at a time, beating after each addition until the mixture is light and fluffy. Beat in the eggs a little at a time until they are well combined. Add the vanilla and pumpkin puree and beat until the mixture is smooth. Stir in the chocolate chips and chopped nuts.

4. Pour the batter into the prepared pan, smoothing the top with a rubber spatula. Bake the bread for 45 to 50 minutes, or until a cake tester inserted in the center comes out clean. Let the bread cool in the pan on a rack for 5 minutes. Remove the bread from the pan and return to the rack to cool completely. Sift confectioners' sugar over the bread before serving.

❖ f i g g y p u d d i n g ❖

YIELD: 2 ONE-QUART PUDDINGS

1/4 cup candied orange peel

1/4 cup brandy or dark rum

1 pound dried figs, chopped

2 cups scalded milk

1 1/2 cups all-purpose flour

2 1/2 teaspoons baking powder

2 1/2 teaspoons cinnamon

1 1/2 teaspoons freshly grated nutmeg

1/2 teaspoon ground cloves

1/2 teaspoon salt

1 cup (2 sticks) unsalted butter, softened

1 cup sugar

3 large eggs

2 teaspoons pure vanilla extract

1 1/2 cups fresh bread crumbs

2 tablespoons grated orange peel

1/2 cup chopped walnuts

Figgy pudding—the very name conjures up visions of sugarplums and Christmases past. If you've never made a Christmas pudding, this is the one to start with. Figs and orange peel, brandy and spices, butter and nuts are all combined in a pretty mold, then gently steamed for two hours. Here is a recipe that hasn't changed in a hundred years, and will probably be made the same way a hundred years hence. If you can find Devonshire or clotted cream at the market, whip it up a bit and serve it alongside thin slices of the pudding.

1. Generously butter two 1-quart decorative pudding molds with fitted lids. In a bowl, toss together the orange peel and brandy and let stand 15 minutes.

2. In a saucepan, combine the figs with the hot milk. Bring the mixture to a boil and simmer, stirring occasionally, for 20 minutes. Let cool.

3. Into a bowl, sift the flour, baking powder, spices, and salt. In a large bowl, cream the butter. Add the sugar a little at a time, and beat the mixture until it is light and fluffy. Add the eggs one at a time, beating well after each addition. Stir in the vanilla. Add the bread crumbs, grated orange peel, walnuts, and the reserved candied orange peel and brandy. Add the flour mixture alternately with the fig mixture, beginning and ending with the flour mixture and beating well after each addition.

4. Pour the batter into the prepared pudding molds and attach the lids. Place each mold on a wire rack in a heavy, deep saucepan. Add enough hot water to reach halfway up the side of the mold. Cover the pans and steam the puddings over medium-low heat for 2 hours, replenishing the water if necessary.

5. Remove the molds from the saucepans. Let the puddings cool, covered, for 15 minutes before unmolding. Or let the puddings cool completely and refrigerate them for up to two weeks. Steam cold puddings for 1 to 1 1/2 hours to reheat.

❖ p a n e t t o n e ❖

YIELD: 2 LOAVES

FOR THE SPONGE

One .25-ounce package active dry yeast

½ cup warm milk

1 cup all-purpose flour

FOR THE DOUGH

⅔ cup currants

⅔ cup dried apricots, coarsely chopped

⅔ cup raisins

¼ cup candied citron

2 tablespoons dark rum

½ cup (1 stick) unsalted butter

½ teaspoon salt

½ cup sugar

3 tablespoons grated orange peel

2 teaspoons pure vanilla extract

3 cups all-purpose flour

4 large eggs, lightly beaten

1 large egg

Fruity, yeasty panettone, the Italian holiday sweet bread, is divine for Christmas breakfast or tea, served with lemon curd, perhaps, or any fruit preserves. Leftover slices are enhanced by toasting.

1. Make the sponge: In a bowl, combine the yeast with the milk and whisk until smooth. Stir in the flour until combined well. Cover with plastic wrap and let rise in a warm place for 30 minutes.

2. Make the dough: In a bowl, toss to combine the currants, apricots, raisins, citron, and rum, and let stand for 10 minutes.

3. In the bowl of an electric mixer set at medium speed, combine the butter, salt, and sugar and beat the mixture for 2 to 3 minutes, or until light. Add the orange peel and vanilla and beat 5 minutes. Alternately add the flour and eggs to the butter mixture, in 3 batches, beginning and ending with the flour, beating until well combined. Add the sponge and beat until the dough is smooth and elastic. Stir in the dried fruit and rum mixture.

4. Generously butter a large bowl. Place the dough in the bowl and turn it to coat the top with butter. Cover the bowl with plastic wrap and a tea towel, and let the dough rise in a warm place until it has doubled in bulk, about 1½ hours.

5. Butter well the inside of two 1-pound coffee cans or 1-quart molds. Line the bottoms with buttered parchment paper. Punch down the dough and divide it between the cans. Cover the cans loosely with tea towels and let the dough rise for 1 hour, or until it has almost doubled.

6. Preheat the oven to 350°F. In a small bowl, beat the egg and 1 teaspoon water. With a sharp knife, score the top of each bread with an X; brush with the egg wash. Bake the breads 40 to 45 minutes, or until a cake tester inserted in the center comes out clean. If the loaves begin to brown too quickly, lay a piece of foil over them. Let cool in the cans on a rack for 5 minutes. Unmold the breads and let cool on their sides completely.

❖ c r a n b e r r y   p e a r   c h u t n e y ❖

YIELD: 6 HALF-PINT JARS

$1/2$ cup cider vinegar

$2 1/2$ cups firmly packed light brown sugar

2 tablespoons grated fresh gingerroot

2 teaspoons cinnamon

$1/2$ teaspoon ground cloves

2 lemons, peel grated, pith discarded, flesh cut into large pieces

1 navel orange, peel grated, pith discarded, flesh cut into large pieces

3 Bosc pears, peeled, cored, and coarsely chopped

3 cups fresh or frozen cranberries

1 cup raisins

Chutneys are such delightful condiments, rich in flavor and chunky in texture by virtue of their spices and fruits. Serve chutney with roasted pork or chicken, on a cheese plate, or with toasted English muffins for an evening snack. Once cooled, the chutney can be stored in the refrigerator for up to two weeks. If you would like to preserve it, follow the directions in the Note below. To include it in a gift basket, prepare a pretty label and cover the jar lid with a square of fabric held in place with kitchen string or satin cord.

1. In a large saucepan, combine the vinegar, sugar, spices, and $1 1/2$ cups water. Bring the mixture to a boil over high heat, stirring, and cook until the sugar dissolves. Add the lemon and orange peels and flesh, and the pears. Simmer the mixture, stirring frequently, for 10 minutes.

2. Add 2 cups of the cranberries and the raisins to the pan and simmer, stirring occasionally, for 35 minutes, or until the chutney has thickened. Stir in the remaining 1 cup cranberries and simmer, stirring frequently, for 15 minutes.

3. Transfer the chutney to a bowl and let it cool. Cover and chill the chutney overnight.

Note: To preserve the chutney, do not allow it to cool. Spoon the hot chutney into 6 sterilized half-pint mason-style jars, filling each jar to within $1/2$ inch of the top. Wipe the rims with a dampened cloth and tightly close the lids. Arrange the jars in a water-bath canner or on a rack in a deep pot and pour in enough hot water to cover the jars by 2 inches. Bring the water to a boil and process, covered, for 10 minutes. Transfer the jars with canning tongs to a rack and allow them to cool. Make certain that the seals are intact. Label the jars and store them in a cool, dark place for up to 3 months.

❖ r o s e m a r y   v i n e g a r ❖

YIELD: 1 QUART

1 quart white wine vinegar

2 large rosemary sprigs, or to taste

Sometimes the most unassuming gifts give the greatest pleasure. A case in point: rosemary vinegar. With the availability of fresh herbs in markets year-round, this rosemary vinegar can be made in early December for Christmas giving. Before using it or giving it as a gift, though, remove the rosemary sprigs and replace them with fresh ones.

In a stainless-steel or enamel saucepan, bring the vinegar to a simmer. Pour it into a sterilized bottle or jar and add 2 sprigs of rosemary or more to taste. Seal the bottle and store it in a cool, dark place for at least 2 weeks.

❖ r a s p b e r r y   v i n e g a r ❖

YIELD: ABOUT 3 CUPS

4 cups red raspberries, divided

3 cups white wine vinegar

1/2 cup sugar

Raspberry vinegar takes a bit more effort to make than rosemary vinegar, but it is worth the effort. Splash it on green beens, rice salads, and potato salads. The vinegar's ruby jewel tone makes it a beautiful gift.

In a bowl, combine 2 cups of the berries and the vinegar and let stand, covered, for 24 hours. Drain, reserving the berries for another use. Add the remaining 2 cups of berries and let stand another 24 hours. Strain the vinegar into a saucepan, add the sugar, and simmer over medium-low heat, stirring occasionally, for 10 minutes. Strain through cheesecloth into hot, sterile bottles and seal.

❖ s p i c e d   a l m o n d s ❖

YIELD: ABOUT 1½ CUPS

2 teaspoons smoked paprika

¼ cup plus 1 teaspoon sugar

½ teaspoon sea salt or coarse salt

½ teaspoon ground cumin

½ teaspoon cayenne pepper

2 tablespoons vegetable oil

1½ cups blanched whole almonds

With cocktails, offer your guests these distinctive, peppery almonds. The secret is the smoked paprika, available at specialty food stores and by mail order. The nuts will keep in an airtight container for up to two weeks.

1. In a large bowl, combine the smoked paprika, 1 teaspoon sugar, the salt, cumin, and cayenne pepper. Set aside.

2. In a large skillet over medium heat, heat the oil. Add the almonds and cook, stirring, until they are golden. Add the remaining sugar and cook, shaking the pan, until the sugar is caramelized and the nuts are a dark golden brown.

3. Transfer the almonds to the bowl containing the spices and stir to coat. Cool the almonds on a nonstick baking sheet.

❖ h e r b - s p i c e d   n u t s ❖

YIELD: ABOUT 3 CUPS

1½ pounds mixed unsalted shelled nuts

3 tablespoons minced fresh rosemary

1 tablespoon sugar

1 tablespoon sea salt or coarse salt

2 teaspoons garlic powder

¾ teaspoon cayenne pepper

3 tablespoons melted unsalted butter

Tasty standbys for entertaining and gift-giving, herb-spiced nuts have a buttery, sweet-salty flavor that is enhanced with a bit of cayenne. Store cooled nuts in an airtight container in the refrigerator for up to two weeks.

1. Preheat the oven to 350°F. Arrange the nuts in a single layer on a jelly-roll pan or a baking sheet. Roast them in the oven for 10 minutes, stirring occasionally.

2. Meanwhile, in a large bowl, combine the rosemary, sugar, salt, garlic powder, and cayenne. Remove the nuts from the oven but do not turn it off. Transfer the hot nuts to the bowl, add the butter, and toss to coat with the spices. Return the nuts to the baking sheet and roast for 10 minutes more. Place the nuts on paper towels and allow to cool completely.

Projects and Patterns

dressy ribbon ornaments

Here's your chance to go dizzyingly overboard at the ribbon store. The only constraints on the designs you can create for these gorgeous ribbon balls, shown on pages 14 and 15 and below, are your own imagination and your supply of materials. Include some 2-inch Styrofoam balls if you want variety of size. To make the ornaments, you will need:

3-inch Styrofoam balls

Assorted ribbons

Sequin pins

As you work, leave the ribbons on their spools. Place the end of a ribbon on a Styrofoam ball and pin in place. Keeping it taut, wrap the ribbon once around the ball, attach it with another sequin pin where it meets itself, and cut (this will be the top of the ornament). Add additional ribbons, attached the same way, beginning and ending at the top, until the ball is covered and you have achieved the desired design. For hanging, pin a loop of ribbon to the top of the ball; use several pins to keep it secure, if necessary.

Hints: Combine ribbons of different textures, patterns, colors, and widths. When using different widths on one ball, start with the wider ribbbons; depending on their width, they may need a few extra pins to gather them at the top and bottom in order to fit the curve of the ball. For a fancy striped effect, layer one or two ribbons of decreasing size directly over a wider ribbon. When making loops for hanging, try using knots and bows at the top or bottom of the loop. Let your creativity get the best of you!

ribbon rosettes

Make these blooms in a monochromatic scheme, perhaps using only satin and grosgrain ribbons, or use several colors and combine textures— jacquards, satins, ruffle-edged organdy, velvet, or ombré. The possibilities, you'll soon discover, are endless, so mix and match to your heart's content. To make rosettes like the ones on page 12 and above, you will need:

Assorted 1-inch-wide ribbons

Assorted 1 1/2-inch-wide ribbons

Miniature ribbon roses

Pin backs, if desired

Glue, if desired

Sewing supplies

1. Make the outer ring of petals: Cut four 9 1/2-inch lengths of 1-inch-wide ribbon. Loop each piece so its ends overlap 1/2 inch, flatten the loop so the overlap is centered at the back, and secure all three layers together with a single stitch. Stack all four loops together as if making an asterisk, and sew them together at the center with several stitches.

2. Make the two inner petals: For the larger petal, cut a 9-inch length of 1 1/2-inch-wide ribbon. Fold it in half lengthwise, and, depending on the weave of the ribbon, sew a 1/16- to 1/8-inch seam along the cut edges to make a loop; press the seam allowance flat. Sew a running stitch, about 1/16 inch in from the edge, all the way around one side of the loop; pull the thread to gather the ribbon into a flower, sew a stitch to secure it, and press it flat with your fingers. For the smaller petal, repeat this process with a 7-inch length of 1-inch-wide ribbon.

3. Assemble the rosette: Center the smaller inner petal over the larger inner petal, and center those on the outer ring of petals. Secure all three pieces together with several stitches at the center. With a stitch or with a dab of glue, attach a ribbon rose to the center of the innermost petal. To add a loop for hanging, cut 1-inch-wide ribbon to the desired length, fold it in half, and stitch the ends to the back of the rosette. To use on a lapel or a hat, glue a pin back to the center of the back of the rosette.

fancy-paper favor cartons

The paper-covered boxes on pages 16 and 17 and above were inspired by vintage candy boxes found at a Paris flea market. To make one, you will need:

One sheet of 11-by-17-inch card stock

One sheet of 11-by-17-inch poster board

One sheet of 11-by-17-inch decorative paper to cover the box, such as wrapping paper, photocopied images, or vintage wallpaper

Two 16-inch lengths of $1/2$-inch- to 1-inch- wide grosgrain ribbon

Three all-purpose plain white 3-by-1$3/4$-inch adhesive-backed labels

Spray glue

Glue

1. On a photocopier, enlarge the two carton patterns on page 136 to 250%. Cut out the patterns and trace them onto card stock. Cut the shape out of the card stock. This will be a template you can use again and again.

2. Trace the box pattern onto the posterboard and cut it out using a utility knife and cutting mat. Trace the small rectangle pattern onto the posterboard, cut it out, and set it aside.

3. To attach the paper covering, spray glue onto the posterboard cut-out and smooth down the paper so it adheres evenly. Let it dry. With a utility knife and cutting mat, trim the excess paper from the posterboard cut-out.

4. With a pencil, lightly mark the score lines on the posterboard side of the cut-out, as indicated by the dotted lines on the template. Fold back along the lines, using a ruler to keep a crisp edge.

5. To attach the ribbon ties, lightly make two pencil marks the width of the ribbon, centering each on a wide side of the box 1 inch from the top, as indicated by the solid lines on the template. With the utility knife, slice all the way through the box sides along each line. Thread about an inch of each ribbon through each slit into the insides of the cut-out. With a generous dab of glue, attach each ribbon to the inside of the cut-out. Let dry. Cover the exposed ribbons on the inside of the cut-out with an adhesive label for a tidy appearance.

6. Fold the posterboard along the scoring marks. Glue the carton closed along the long tab. Fold the bottom ends along the scoring lines, seal closed with an adhesive label, and place the posterboard rectangle in the bottom of the inside of the box for added support. Fold the top along the scoring marks. Fill the box with treats or little gifts, close the flaps, and tie the ribbons into a bow to close.

fanned cuff stocking

The velvet-trimmed stocking on page 18 and below is most beautiful when made with a shimmering solid-color or softly iridescent fabric. A small- to medium-scale pattern—perhaps a toile—would also work nicely. Avoid plaids or stripes, as they would not show the flared cuff to its best advantage. To make the stocking, you will need:

$1/2$ yard of fabric, such as silk charmeuse or dupioni

$1/2$ yard of iron-on stiffening material, if needed

4 feet of $3/8$- to $1/2$-inch-wide velvet ribbon

Sewing supplies

1. With a photocopier, enlarge the pattern on page 136 to 250% (or adjust it to the size you wish) and cut it out.

2. If you have a supple fabric such as silk charmeuse, iron the stiffening material to the wrong side of the fabric to help it hold its shape.

3. Fold the fabric in half, right sides facing. Pin the pattern to the fabric, then cut out both panels of the stocking.

4. With right sides facing, pin the panels together $1/4$ inch from the edges. Sew a $1/4$-inch seam around the perimeter of the stocking, leaving the cuff open.

5. So seams will lie smoothly, clip notches in fabric at curved edges, to about $1/16$ inch from the seam. Turn the stocking right side out and press flat with a medium-hot iron.

6. Finish the cuff: Turn down the fabric $1/4$ inch, wrong sides facing, and press. Turn down the fabric $1/4$ inch again and press. Sew a hem all the way around the cuff (this hem will be covered by the ribbon). Fold the ribbon in half and position its midpoint at the front of the cuff. Along the bottom edge of the ribbon, sew it all the way around the cuff so that it covers the hem. Add a few extra stitches at the back of the cuff for strength. Tie the tails of the ribbon in a knot or bow, for hanging.

flouncy cuff stocking

We like this slender stocking—*page 19 and below*—*in a luxurious solid silk. To further accentuate its length, you could use a ribbed silk faille or a narrow stripe running cuff to heel. To make the stocking, you will need:*

½ yard of fabric, such as silk charmeuse or dupioni

½ yard of iron-on stiffening material, if needed

Wide flouncy trim or extra-wide sturdy fancy ribbon

Sewing supplies

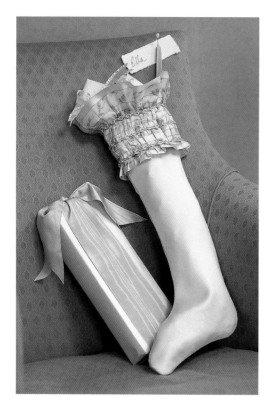

1. With a photocopier, enlarge the pattern on page 137 to 200% (or adjust it to the size you wish) and cut it out.

2. If you have a supple fabric such as silk charmeuse, iron the stiffening material to the wrong side of the fabric to help it hold its shape.

3. Fold the fabric in half, right sides facing. Pin the pattern to the fabric, then cut out both panels of the stocking.

4. With right sides facing, pin the panels together ¼ inch from the edge. Sew a ¼-inch seam around the perimeter of the stocking, leaving the cuff open.

5. So the seams will lie smoothly, clip notches in the fabric at the curved edges, to about ¹⁄₁₆ inch from stitching. Turn right side out and press flat with a medium-hot iron.

6. Finish the cuff: Turn down the fabric ¼ inch, wrong sides facing, and press. Turn down the fabric ¼ inch again and press. Sew a hem all the way around the cuff (this hem will be covered by the ribbon). Starting at the center back of the stocking, measure trim to fit the cuff, adding ¼ inch on each end for a seam allowance, and cut. Turn the trim to the wrong side, pin together ¼ inch in from the cut edges, and stitch. Turn the trimming back to the right side, slip it over the cuff, and stitch it to the stocking.

7. To create a loop for hanging, cut a 14-inch length of ribbon, fold it in half, and stitch both ends to the inside of the back of the cuff.

stitched paper stocking

The versatile paper stockings on pages 44 and 45 and above can be made using sturdy solid or patterned paper for the front panel or for both panels—just skip the color photocopying in Step 2. To make the stockings as shown, you will need:

Images such as snapshots, wallpaper, a page
    from a book, poems, or children's drawings

Removable tape

Card stock

1/4-inch hole punch

Wax-coated twine, narrow ribbon, or yarn

1. With a photocopier, enlarge the pattern on page 137 to 150% (or adjust it to the size you wish) and cut it out.

2. Use a color photocopier to copy the images you wish to place on the stocking. Cut them out to fit the paper stocking pattern and attach them with removable tape applied to the wrong side so it won't show. Make a color photocopy of the finished design and cut it out.

3. For the back panel of the stocking, trace the template onto card stock and cut it out.

4. Holding the two panels of the stocking together, punch holes around the perimeter, about 1/4 inch to 3/4 inch apart, but not across the cuff.

5. Lace the two sides of the stocking together with twine, ribbon, or yarn, with a whipstitch or a running stitch, depending upon the look you prefer. Begin and end by making knots in the ends of the twine to anchor them at the back of the top holes at the shin and calf of the stocking.

6. To create a loop for hanging, cut a length of twine, ribbon, or yarn, thread it through the top loop at the calf of the cuff, and tie it closed.

Hint: For different looks, cut the cuff in an overscale zigzag, or use pinking shears, scallop shears, or decorative-edge paper scissors, perhaps one with a wavy edge. You can also add a separate paper cuff: Before lacing the panels together, cut a 2-inch-wide strip of patterned paper to fit as a cuff; punch holes to align with the holes in the stocking, then lace the stocking.

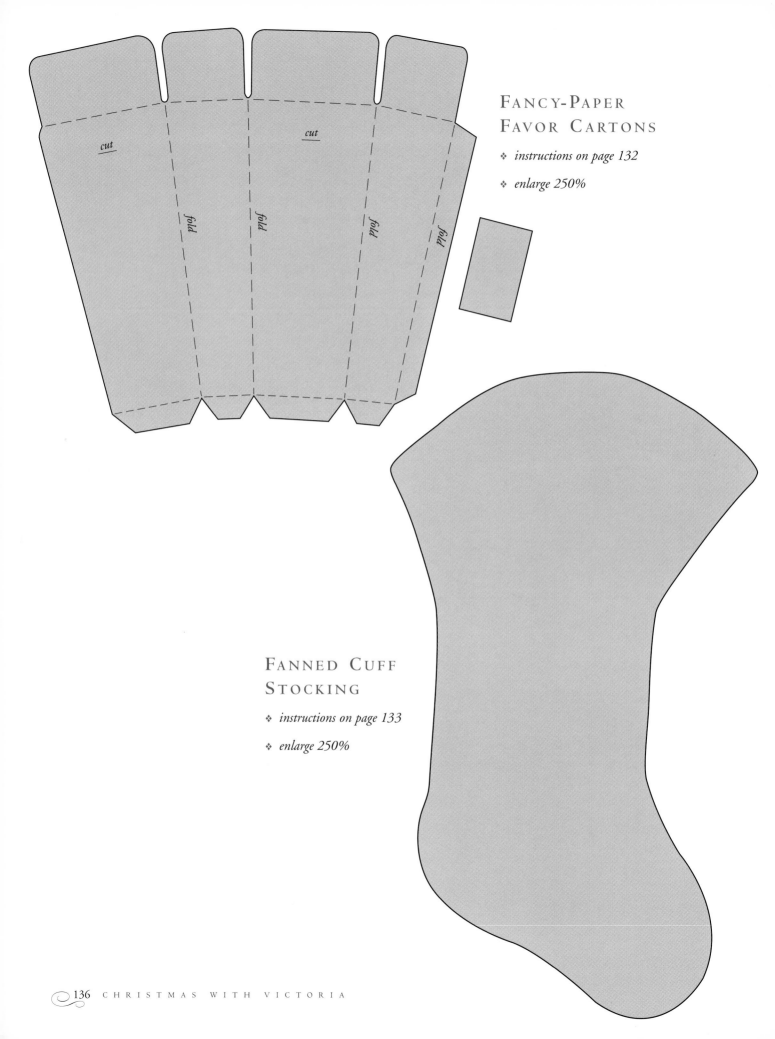

FANCY-PAPER
FAVOR CARTONS

❖ *instructions on page 132*

❖ *enlarge 250%*

cut

cut

fold

fold

fold

fold

FANNED CUFF
STOCKING

❖ *instructions on page 133*

❖ *enlarge 250%*

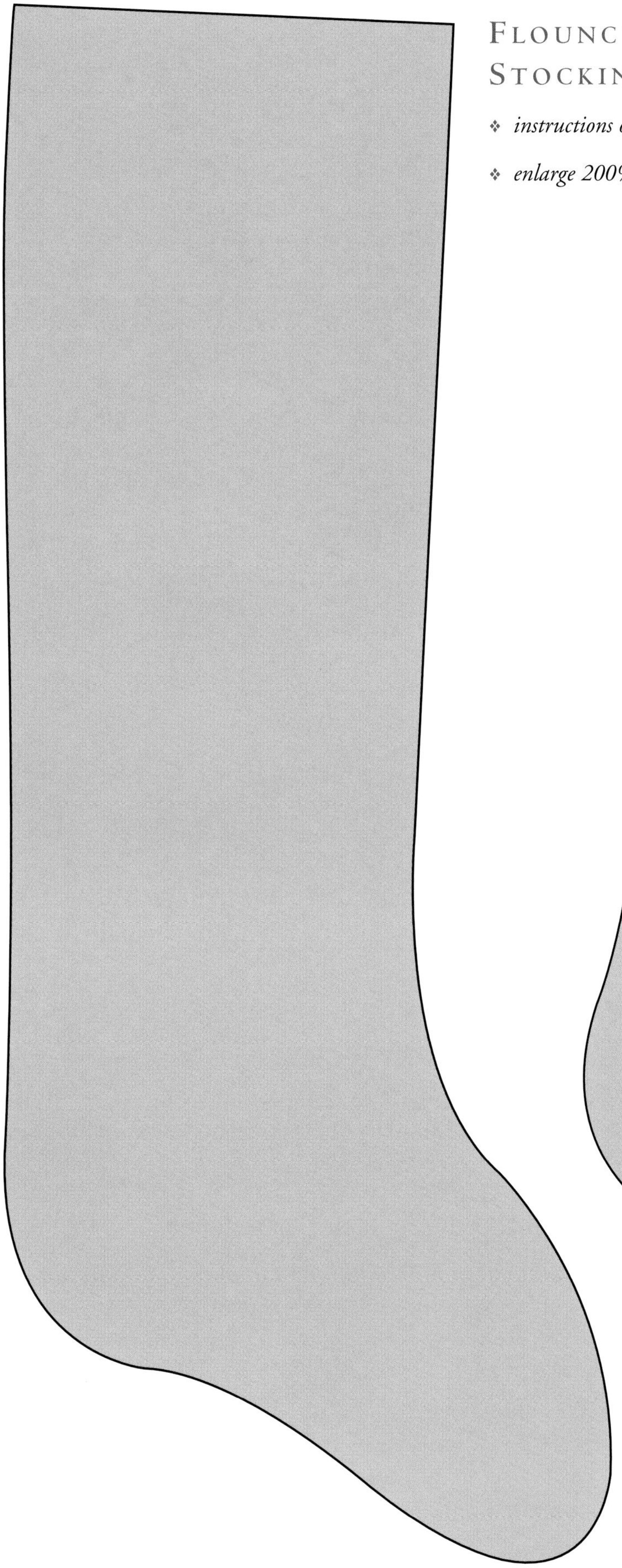

FLOUNCY CUFF
STOCKING

❖ *instructions on page 134*

❖ *enlarge 200%*

STITCHED PAPER
STOCKING

❖ *instructions on page 135*

❖ *enlarge 150%*

Resources

The following is a chapter-by-chapter listing of sources for as many of the items pictured in this book as possible. Every effort has been made to ensure the accuracy of addresses, telephone numbers, Websites, and e-mail addresses, but these may change prior to or after publication.

ALL THE TRIMMINGS

page 10

Assorted ribbons and *pink pleated rice paper* from Mokuba, 55 West 39th Street, New York, NY 10018; (212) 869-8900.

pages 10, 11

Bandbox ornaments from Hannah's Treasures, 1101 Seventh Street, Harlan, IA 51537; (877) 643-2512 or (712) 755-3173 or www.hannahstreasures.com.

page 12 (bottom)

Esquire reversible quilted silk throw from Rural Residence, 316 Warren Street, Hudson, NY 12534; (518) 822-9259 or www.ruralresidence.com.

page 15

19th-century Louis XV–style gilt fauteuil from Doyle Antiques, 714 Warren Street, Hudson, NY 12534; (518) 828-3929.

Blue spruce from Roxbury Hollow Farm, 226 Old Barrington Road, Hudson, NY 12534; (518) 851-8922.

Metal garden urn from Botanicus Antiques and Fine Arts, 446 Warren Street, Hudson, NY 12534; (518) 828-0520.

New painted cabriole-legged table from Benjamin Wilson Antiques, 513 Warren Street, Hudson, NY 12534; (518) 822-0866.

Bandbox ornaments and *large bandboxes* from Hannah's Treasures, see above.

Assorted ribbons on gifts from
Mokuba, see above, and from
Tinsel Trading Co., 47 West 38th
Street, New York, NY 10018;
(212) 730-1030.

Assorted papers on gifts from
Mokuba, see above, and from
New York Central Art Supply,
62 Third Avenue, New York,
NY 10003; (212) 477-0400.

page 17 (bottom)
Evening bags from Metropolitan
Design Group, (212) 944-6110.

pages 20, 21
Mother-of-pearl buttons from
Jo-Ann Fabrics and Crafts,
(888) 739-4120 or www.joann.com.

"Penpal" wallpaper in background
from Waverly, (800) 423-5881.

Square dish from Gracious Home,
1220 Third Avenue, New York,
NY 10021; (212) 517-6300 or
www.gracioushome.com.

Ruffle-edged linen towels, straw tray,
and soap dishes from Gracious Home,
see above.

Apothecary jars from Restoration
Hardware, (800) 762-1005 or
www.restorationhardware.com.

pages 24, 25
Antique oval gilt mirror
from Doyle Antiques,
714 Warren Street, Hudson,
NY 12534; (518) 828-3929.

New painted lyre-pedestal table
from Benjamin Wilson Antiques,
513 Warren Street, Hudson,
NY 12534; (518) 822-0866.

Five-inch pink satin ribbon
from Mokuba, 55 West 39th Street,
New York, NY 10018;
(212) 869-8900.

French crystal Champagne
flutes, pale blue candles, and
Esquire reversible quilted
silk throw from Rural Residence,
see above.

19th-century Louis XV–style
gilt side chair from
Doyle Antiques, see above.

pages 44, 45
White chocolate teddy bear
from Dean & Deluca,
560 Broadway,
New York, NY 10012;
(800) 999-0306 or
www.deananddeluca.com.

page 46 (top)
Rubber stamp (does not
include artwork) from
Airline Stationery Company,
284 Madison Avenue, New York,
NY 10007; (212) 532-6525 or
www.airlineinc.com.

page 46 (bottom)
Miniature knit Christmas stocking
from Midwest of Cannon Falls,
32057 64th Avenue,
Cannon Falls, MN 55009;
(800) 548-8696 or
www.midwestofcannonfalls.com.

page 47
Handmade candy canes from
Altamarie Candy Company,
(800) 721-7714 or
www.candycornerusa.com.

page 54 (top)

Ribbon from Offray Ribbon,
(800) 363-3729.

Wheat weaving by Patricia Kehoe
DeVries, available through
Christkindlmarkt, Bethlehem, PA;
(610) 861-0678 or www.fest.org.

pages 54, 55

Candles from Partylite,
(508) 830-3100 or www.partylite.com.

Hurricane lamps and *glass cylinders*
from Aero, (888) 814-7988.

page 57

Mirrored star sconce from
Old Salem, 730 South Poplar Street,
Winston-Salem, NC 27101;
(800) 822-5151 or www.oldsalem.org.

Beeswax ornaments from Cinnamon
Treasures Apiaries, (302) 684-8619.

page 58

Moravian star ornament from
Pennsylvania German Folk Art Papers,
(610) 779-8423.

Pinecone beeswax ornament from
Beeswax Bunnies, (919) 735-9501.

Terra-cotta heart ornament
by Pamela Iobst, (610) 437-4743.

page 60 (right)

*Handmade paper with chicken
wire* from Kate's Paperie,
561 Broadway, New York, NY
10012; (212) 941-9816 or
www.katespaperie.com.

page 61

Translucent ball ornaments from
Thames Glass, Newport, RI; (401)
846-0576 or www.thamesglass.com.

Gold- and silver-plated ornaments
from Carrie Fertig, (518) 851-7826.

Wheat garlands from Swe-Den Inc.,
(800) 487-9333.

Colored teardrop ornaments from
Elias Studios, (508) 252-6954.

Star atop tree from Ed Torr,
The Tin Tinker, (215) 529-0962.

page 62

*Number 102 Pandan rattan boxes
(square, in acorn)* from Via Motif,
(415) 454-8842 or www.viamotif.com.

page 64 (top)

Napkins from Kim Seybert, 20 West
33rd Street, 11th Floor, New York,
NY 10001; (212) 564-7850 or
www.kimseybert.com.

Curtain used as tablecloth from
Mastro Raphaël, 225 Fifth Avenue,
Showroom 706, New York,
NY 10010; (212) 448-1965 or
www.mastroraphael.com.

page 64 (bottom)

Basket from Coco Co.
at William Laman, (805) 969-2840
or www.williamlaman.com.

pages 64–66

"Saumar Truffle" clear-glass vase from Un Jardin En Plus, 20224 South Normandy, Torrence, CA 90502; (310) 768-8170.

page 65

Large bowl ("Peony"), medium bowl ("Rustic"), and *small bowl ("Eggshell")* from Middle Kingdom, (202) 338-4910.

Napkins from ABH Designs, 160 East 56th Street, 10th Floor, New York, NY 10022; (212) 688-3764.

pages 66, 67

"Merlot" crystal decanter from Galleri Orrefors Kosta Boda, 685 Madison Avenue, New York, NY 10021; (212) 752-1095 or www.orrefors.com or www.kostaboda.com.

Hunslet creamware serving plate (shown with tart) and *"Plain Lattice" platter* from Hartley Greens & Co., 011-44-1347-878-433 or www.worldwideshoppingmall.co.uk/potteryshop.

"Laurel Swag" glasses from Design Workshop, P.O. Box 451, Warsaw, NC 28398; (910) 293-7329.

Stacked "Gingham" dessert plates and *salad bowl* from Fioriware, 333 Market Street, Zanesville, OH 43701; (740) 454-7400 ext. 12 or www. fioriware.com.

Apothecary jar used as vase from Manorisms, 73 Northwyke, Jackson, TN 38305; (901) 660-8802 or www.manorisms.com.

Green bowl from Nikolas Weinstein Studios, 1649 Valencia Street, San Francisco, CA 94110; (415) 643-5418 or www.nikolas.net.

page 69

Napkins in glasses from Triangle Studios, (800) 820-4707.

page 70

"Strawberry Basket" pierced-rim creamware platter from Hartley Greens & Co., see above.

page 71

"Cyrano" crystal cake pedestal from Galleri Orrefors Kosta Boda, see above.

Antique silver cake server from The Country Dining Room Antiques, 178 Main Street, Great Barrington, MA 01230; (413) 528-5050 or www.countrydiningroomantiq.com.

WINTER
FEASTS

page 72

Glazed pears from De Choix Specialty Food, Woodside, NY; (718) 507-8080.

page 73

French faience soup tureen with flower finial from A La Maison, 1078 Madison Avenue, New York, NY 10028; (212) 396-1020.

page 76

"Melon Terrine and Ladle" (at left) and *covered bowl (at center)* from Hartley Greens & Co. at Leeds Pottery, 011-44-1347-878-433 or www.worldwideshoppingmall.co.uk/ potteryshop.

"Ivoire" bone china tureen (at right) from the Château Collection of Villeroy & Boch, (800) 845-5376.

page 77 (bottom left)

"Fruits and Flowers" soup plate from Herend, (800) 643-7363 or www.herendusa.com.

page 80

All tableware from Constance Maupin, Paris; 011-33-1-43-07-01-28.

page 81

Glazed pears from De Choix Specialty Food, see above.

GIFTS FROM
THE KITCHEN

page 86

Glass urn with gold ribbon from Manorisms, 73 Northwyke, Jackson, TN 38305; (901) 660-8802 or www.manorisms.com.

page 88

White ceramic pie plates from Sur La Table, (800) 243-0852 or www.surlatable.com.

Rattan box from Via Motif, (415) 454-8842 or www.viamotif.com.

page 89

Bamboo steamer with handle from Pearl River, 277 Canal Street, New York, NY 10013; (212) 431-4770.

Six-inch tart dish from Broadway Panhandler, 477 Broome Street, New York, NY 10013; (212) 966-3434 or www.broadwaypanhandler.com.

Berry tart from Brandow's and Co., 340 Warren Street, Hudson, NY 12534; (518) 822-8938.

page 91

Pie plate and *fluted pudding mold* from Sur La Table, see above.

French wire bowl from Coco Co. at William Laman, (805) 969-2840 or www.williamlaman.com.

page 92 (bottom)

Gold tins from Broadway Panhandler, see above.

page 94

Italian canning jars from Sur La Table, see above.

Bleached basket from Modulus, (800) 486-2580.

page 95

Reproduction refrigerator dishes from Restoration Hardware, (800) 762-1005 or www.restorationhardware.com.

page 96 (bottom)

Fluted crystal glass from William Yeoward Crystal, (800) 818-8484 or www.williamyeowardcrystal.com.